Hack Proof

Hack Proof

*Protecting Your Privacy and Personal Data in
the Digital Economy*

John Berry

Big Sky, Florida

ISBN 978-0-9966012-0-7 paperback edition

ISBN 978-0-9966012-1-4 e-book edition

Printed by CreateSpace, An Amazon.com Company

A "how-to" guide for those who recognize the importance of securing their data and their privacy in the digital economy.

Hack Proof – Protecting Your Privacy and Personal Data in the Digital Economy

Table of Contents

Introduction

"The Internet is the first thing that humanity has built that humanity doesn't understand, it's the largest experiment in anarchy that we have ever had."
Eric Schmidt, Executive Chairman, Google

Hacked and Exposed

The New York Post headline read, "Teen says he hacked CIA director's AOL account".[1] "No way!" I'm sure that I, along with many others who work in cyber security all thought it was highly unlikely. How can we expect anyone to secure their email and data accounts if CIA Director John Brennan wasn't able to? However, over the next few days, the details spilled out. A teen hacker and his friends had used simple social engineering to trick Verizon into giving up vital personal information on John Brennan. The hacker and his friends then used this information to access and reset the password on Director Brennan's personal AOL email account. They also posted some confidential information online they had uncovered and then phoned and taunted him on his mobile phone.

So at the same time as Presidential candidate Hilary Clinton's naive use of a personal email server to send highly sensitive and top secret work was being exposed in the media, we learned that the head of the Central Intelligence Agency was doing the same thing! That both of these high-profile individuals made simple mistakes and were found out should hopefully be a wake-up call to many.

The fact is, it's scary easy to be hacker today. There are so many free tools, books, websites, forums, and online videos that anyone with simple skills and time can target you for any reason.

P.S. Note to Clinton and Brennan: "security-by-obscurity" (hoping no one will find or bother with your personal email) is not a secure strategy!

Why I Wrote this Book

The world is more connected than at any other time in human history. We are all ensconced in an immersive digital blanket that surrounds the earth. Never before have so many people been able to connect with almost anyone from anywhere with so much ease.

Yet while the Internet has benefitted billions of people with access to information—the ability to communicate, conduct online transactions, and view entertainment—there is a huge dark side as the opening story so clearly reveals. The very technologies we are using to get online, including our smartphones and the burgeoning everything connected, Internet-of-Things (IoT) ecosystem, are perfect spy tools as it turns out. As we go about our daily lives, every minute of each day government agencies and businesses of all sizes are using technology devices to keep track of us and reach deeper into our lives. This Orwellian-like collection of personal data and the surveillance of private citizens is a global problem that's growing bigger by the day. Terabytes of new data are generated as we go about our normal everyday lives. All of our very personal data is being collected, sorted, and analyzed by big brother agencies along with thousands of private data brokers and commercial firms utilizing surveillance-as-a-business model. We are all being profiled in great detail in hundreds of big data systems. Mostly this is happening without our explicit knowledge, even if in some cases we may have been tricked into giving our consent.

Likewise as CIA Director Brennan now knows from first-hand experience, cyber crime and computer hacking are booming. Every second of everyday, somewhere in the world 15 people are having their identity stolen. Numerous malware and hacking attacks of all kinds are wreaking havoc, stealing information and infecting systems and devices in increasing numbers. The more we get connected, the bigger the attack surface becomes. The costs to both individuals and businesses run into billions annually with no end in sight. Unlike many tragedies and disasters that make news headlines, cyber crime is not happening half-a-world away in some developing nation. It is at our front door, occurring right here in our homes and cites, affecting our families, friends, and neighbors.

Actionable Information

Anyone interested in the two main overlapping topics of privacy and data security can easily find more information online on each subject than they can handle. That, however, is part of the problem. We are drowning in information. Some of it is accurate, some less so, some current, and a lot outdated.

For the non-security or non-privacy professional, it's difficult to know what information and solutions to apply. If securing your data and privacy was as easy as simply doing some online reading, we wouldn't have the high levels of identity theft and fraud we see happening. We also wouldn't be witnessing as many victims of malware attacks as we do. Even with so much available information, non-security professionals are distrustful of some of the best security tools. Essential tools such as password managers are mistakenly overlooked. There is an over-reliance on other tools like anti-virus solutions, and users neglect the vital task of updating and patching their systems.

Likewise with privacy protection, (especially since the Edward Snowden NSA revelations), many articles, media reports, and books have been written that do a good job of describing the problems. However, most are aimed at security

17

and privacy professionals, and less so at regular working professionals and young adults who live online. This book is written for the millions of non-technical, everyday computer users. They are often the victims of cyber crime, invasive data collection from online companies, and over-reaching of personal information from government agencies.

Who This Book Will Benefit

While the information contained in this book will benefit anyone interested in increased privacy and security, there are certain people in particular who will gain from it. As more people become aware of just how much data is being collected about them, the list will continue to grow. This book is for all of these people:

- Anyone who has been the victim of identity theft or fraud will benefit from the solutions offered.

- Anyone who has been the victim of stalking or abuse will be better able to protect their data and privacy for both themselves and their family.

- Anyone who has been the victim of "doxxing" (the intentional public exposure of personal details in order to facilitate the harassment of the victim, including threats of violence) needs to protect their data.

- Anyone who may find themselves in the media spotlight for whatever reason needs to understand how to protect their data and privacy.

- Public figures who wish to retain some level of personal privacy for themselves and their families.

- Those in law enforcement and their families need to take steps to protect themselves and their data and ensure they can't be tracked by down by criminals.

- Those in the military and their families need to protect their private data and ensure their families can't be tracked down. In March 2015, the brutal Islamic State called upon its members and followers to attack U.S. military personnel at their homes. It posted images of service members, their addresses and other contact details, all collected from various public databases, probably people search sites and social media.[2]

- Those who work in the media, reporters, political dissidents, and anyone else who needs to communicate in private and remain anonymous will benefit from taking steps to secure their data.

- Those with over nosy employers, work colleagues, and neighbors who want to keep their lives private.

- Anyone who feels threatened over his or her political or religious beliefs. Politically correct groups and those that don't agree with you have the ability to find and track you easier than ever before. This book will help you stay ahead of them.

- Anyone who values their privacy and wants to communicate in private without all their personal discussions being recorded.

- Lastly, those who simply don't want their personal information harvested and sold by commercial entities, especially without their permission.

Unlike many books that discuss the problems of surveillance, data privacy, and online security, **I want you to take action**, to learn to be better stewards of your own privacy and to be able to protect your data.

The book is laid out as follows:

The early chapters 1 to 5 involve understanding the threats and details around who is collecting your personal information, how and why.

From chapter 5 onward there are **"Action Steps"** segments after many sections of text where technologies, cyber crime, or issues are discussed. These are included so you can take practical action to protect yourself and help your friends and family do the same.

Depending on your knowledge level and available time, using the table of contents at the front of the book you can jump directly to sections or topics that apply to the devices and applications you use most. Once you have read these sections and applied the suggested fixes and/or added the recommended solutions, you can then go back and read through the rest of the book.

For Those Who Just Want to Take Action

If you don't care about the why and who is tracking you and you just want to secure yourself, jump ahead to Chapter 6 (Cyber Crime chapter). After most sections, you will see a "Action Steps" list detailing instructions to protect your privacy or secure your systems from common attacks.

You can always go back and read the rest of the book later.

Throughout the book I'll be discussing and recommending numerous security and technology products. There are many other solutions available. The ones I mention are just to give you an idea and are the products I like or use. *(At the time of this writing, I don't have a financial stake in any of the companies mentioned or receive anything in return for recommending them.)*

I would like to point out that while many of them are freeware and open-source, there is a cost attached to all software development. Many volunteers give their time to help develop the products millions use for free. I would highly recommend supporting the developers and communities that maintain and improve these solutions. Most have "donate" buttons, so please go ahead and send them some money.

For many free products, there are often more advanced paid-for solutions available. In most cases, I would choose the advanced paid-for option. If you value your privacy and the security of your data, it's best not to be too thrifty in this area. If in doubt, it can be a sobering exercise to see that most of us spend much more on coffee and bottled water than we do on securing our data and privacy!

Chapter 1

You Are Being Watched

"We are watching you!"
24 (TV serial drama)

"I'm worried about how we're just a blink technologically away from becoming a totalitarian state, where our government is watching us all the time."
Ladar Levison, founder of Lavabit & founding partner of Dark Mail Alliance

Internet surveillance and online censorship is a global threat to more people than ever before. In China, a new system being implemented by the government uses a social credit score to rank all civilian lives. Unlike the credit scoring system in the USA and elsewhere, in China you lose points for posting comments critical of the government or being friends with someone who does. [3]

While we are not at that level in the USA or Europe yet, we are all under more digital surveillance than ever before. Freedom House, an independent watchdog organization dedicated to the expansion of freedom around the world, tracks big brother surveillance. According to their findings, between May 2013 and May 2014, 41 countries passed or proposed legislation to penalize legitimate forms of online speech. [4]

We live in a fast changing world. This is nowhere more apparent than when we look at the technology all around us that we simply take for granted. Unfortunately, many of the technologies that we use and benefit from every day are the same technologies that are used to track, hack, and spy on us. So if you have ever had a feeling that you were being watched, you are probably correct.

Two of the greatest technology innovations in recent times, the Internet and the mobile phone, have turned from being the perfect communication tools into ever-present surveillance devices. Likewise, as so-called "smart" devices expand into every area of our homes, cars, and cities, our lives will literally be under surveillance 24 hours a day by dozens of sensors. This is not what we thought we were getting into when we all plunged into the current digital, Internet connected tsunami we all live in.

So while smart Internet connected devices and applications bring many benefits to our daily lives, we need to be more aware of the manufacturer's data collection practices and what they do with our data. There is a reason for those long, legal user agreements that no one but the lawyers who wrote them ever read. Put simply, we have all agreed to technology companies collecting our data and spying on us, even if we didn't realize it at the time.

Every day while online, we leave behind enormous amounts of personal data. This data is like breadcrumbs that are sucked up by numerous business and social media entities. The same occurs as we drive our cars and go to the mall or the office. We are creating a personal information trail that most people, until very recently, never thought much about. However, just like an individual piece of a jigsaw puzzle has little value on its own, collect enough pieces and a picture starts to emerge. The same is true with the little pieces of personal information we leave all over the place as we interact with our world. On its own, one little crumb of information doesn't reveal much about us. However, once you gather and combine several pieces, a detailed picture of who we are, our habits and preferences, starts to appear. Gather enough data and not only has your perceived online anonymity disappeared, but your choices can be predicted and you are open to being manipulated.

Welcome to the brave new world of constant surveillance and big data profiling courtesy of the government and big business—the data brokering industry, social media, technology companies, and just about everyone you buy anything from.

The Perfect Storm

As digital technology continues to become more embedded in every area of our lives, the more invasive it becomes. In a nutshell, I believe we are facing a perfect storm of data insecurity and lack of privacy due to several converging factors:

- The Internet is unsecure by default. It was never designed to be a totally locked down secure place to conduct secure transactions and store data in the cloud. It was designed to be a distributed, open network—a trusted environment where researchers and the military could freely share information with other people that they trusted. We are all trying to use the Internet for something it was never designed for. That's part of the problem we face. When you connect everyone and everything, you lose privacy and you give anyone, anywhere, the ability to hack you.

- The digital economy is wonderful; we all love the technology and gadgets. We spend billions on them and will continue to do so. This fact is a driving force for innovation and development among manufacturers and designers of consumer electronics, household appliances, cars, and just about everything else. Internet connectivity and smartphone apps are being added wherever possible. The major problem in this equation, however, is that most of these manufactures and businesses know very little about cyber security. It is simply not their core focus or expertise. In general they think it can be added as an afterthought. The result is that most Internet-of-Things (IoT) devices are and will continue to be far from secure. The hacks will be bad when they come.

- Out of control cyber crime. Almost weekly, large company hacks expose our personal information to cyber criminals. At this stage it's almost safe to assume that someone, somewhere has stolen your personal information. In 2014, half of all American adults had their information exposed due to data breaches.

- Data brokers of every kind are over-collecting consumer data just because they can. This unregulated, in the shadows business, has been going on for years. Today, the data brokering industry is worth billions of dollars, aided by lobbyists who ensure no one stops the unscrupulous bulk collection of our personal data. At the same time far too many people are sharing too much personal information online—totally oblivious of who is looking at and collecting their data.

- There are too many unsecure connected devices and applications. Huge numbers of unsecure online devices, smartphones, tablets, and applications are playing into the hands of cyber criminals ready to take advantage of unaware consumers. While it's the big company hacks that get all the press, it's actually the hundreds of unpatched vulnerabilities that make devices unsecure and open holes to be attacked.

- Unrestricted government surveillance—worldwide law enforcement and national intelligence agencies are investing in an ever-increasing range of surveillance technologies. Everyone (those under suspicion and those who are totally innocent) is being swept up into the same dragnets. This ongoing bulk collection of personal data is sold to gullible politicians who are told this is necessary to keep everyone safe.

Taking Responsibility

There are solutions to many of these issues, but they won't happen on their own. You have to decide to take control and do something, because if you don't there is no one else who will do it for you. If you are serious about keeping your personal data private and secure you will need to change some of your habits and behavior and take responsibility for your own cyber security. That's what the rest of this book is about.

Chapter 2:

Why This All Matters

"Even if we are not doing anything wrong, you are being watched and recorded and the storage and intelligence gathering capabilities of these systems increases every year by orders of magnitude."
NSA whistle blower, Edward Snowden

"Americans are naïve. They are so comfortable with their lives, they need to wake up!"
Leading Romanian cyber criminal/hacker in "The Most Dangerous Town on The Internet" documentary

The world has changed and there is a battle for your personal data. It's more valuable than you know, and you have already given away more than you realize. The more we are being watched, tracked, and profiled, the more it's starting to bother a lot of people.

If too many people lose confidence in the Internet and mobile technology due to pervasive surveillance, they will start to back away from using it. This form of self-censorship would be a huge loss. The Internet and technology should help in making the world a smaller and safer place—a world where we are able to discover and share without the creepy feeling we are being watched, tracked, and profiled.

So before we go any further, it's probably a good idea to explore and defuse some of the most common myths around privacy, cyber security, and surveillance.

Those who benefit from the collection and resale of your private data often tout these myths. From there they often end up in the media and next thing you know, your neighbor is repeating them to you. As a society we need to push back or else nothing will change.

It's not normally necessary to explain to anyone why data security is important. However, when it comes to privacy, too many are willing or believe they have to give up their privacy to gain security. This is just not true.

Privacy and Security Myths

Myth #1: **Only those with something to hide are interested in privacy**

This myth is also often stated as—if you have nothing wrong, you have nothing to hide. This myth is based on a total misunderstanding of what privacy is all about. Privacy is not about having something to hide, privacy is about protecting our fundamental freedoms and liberty, of being able to go places without being followed, pursue interests and take part in life without being tracked and recorded.

Throughout the history of civilization, privacy was a natural right in free societies and absent in those where people were enslaved. In most just societies, laws have protected the right to privacy. Today technology has outstripped legislation, and both big brother and big businesses have taken advantage of this fact to overreach in collecting our data and breaching our privacy.

Those who favor or are engaged in online surveillance usually advocate this myth. It also gets picked up by the friendly talking heads in the media and even finds its way into everyday conversations with our friends and families.

An individual might argue that they don't care about privacy because they have nothing to hide. This would be like saying that you don't really care about freedom of expression because you are not a speaker or writer. Or you don't care about freedom of religion because you are not a worshipper. However, once you start to lose basic freedoms, it's very hard to ever get them back. They fall like dominos.

Another problem with this myth is that everyone has parts of their lives they wish to keep private. That's why we have locks on our doors and drapes on our windows. We share our secrets only with our spouses or closest friends. This is not because we have something to hide, but rather because our personal matters are not for everyone to know. Everyone has information they don't want disclosed to the whole world. Any personal information can be sensitive information depending on the context in which it is used.

For those who don't think they have anything to hide, I wonder how they would feel about sharing their user name and password to their email, phone, and social media accounts. If they have nothing to hide then they should have no problem with anyone reading all their emails and private messages. In reality we all need and desire privacy in our lives.

Myth #2: **No one cares about privacy anymore**

This myth is often heard from leaders in big businesses, like data brokers and social media companies, who make a fortune out of collecting and selling private information and online advertising. It's self-serving and a blatant lie.

The fact is that the main business model of most social media and data brokering businesses is not about protecting your privacy. The heart of their business involves surveillance, tracking, mining, collecting, and selling your data. They are just trying to get you to agree with them.

In truth most people care about their privacy. There are millions of victims of identity theft and tax refund fraud annually. If you ask one of them about the importance of their privacy, they will have much to say! Or you could simply look at the May 2015 Pew study on American's Attitudes about Privacy, Security, and Surveillance. 93% of U.S. adults had very strong views on the importance of privacy in their everyday lives.[5] Similar studies in Europe have also shown that the majority of individuals are concerned about their online data and loss of privacy.

Myth #3: **Privacy is already dead, so it's a waste of time to even try to attain it**

Similar to myth #1, this is another over-used sound bite, loved by technology executives. Judging by the current level of interest in privacy with the numerous debates regarding legislation and protecting user information, we can conclude that this myth is not true. At the moment, there are more people talking about privacy than ever before. There's definitely also more interest from governments and big business around the issue of privacy. While we have lost a lot of our information into big data systems, by changing our habits, investing in security, and limiting how we share data, we can make a big difference to our future privacy. Privacy is only dead when we stop fighting for it.

Myth #4: **The myth of anonymity and de-identification**

Many online businesses, data brokers, and most social media companies have helped to perpetuate this myth. They know it's the only way to share personal information collected from their clients and users without totally freaking everyone out.

It works like this: your personal information is collected by a data broker from numerous sources—a subscription you took out, a service you signed up for, a store loyalty card, a trip booked online, etc. All the information from your transactions and interactions with the company ends up being supplied to one or more data brokers who then trade your information to others who may not have that particular information about you yet. They all build profiles on you, including very real information on who you are, what you like, habits and interests, in some cases possible medical issues, your religious and political views, and more. They then sell this information to advertisers so they can try to sell you more stuff.

This is how the myth works. Before they sell your information they "anonymize" it. In other words they remove some personal identifiable information. They either hash the data (hide it) or they remove it. They tell everyone that you can't be identified from the data they have provided. In their terms it has been de-identified. Herein lies the problem. Numerous studies (Paul Ohm from Georgetown University, Arvind Narayanan and Edward Felton from Princeton, Hui Zang and Jean Bolot, Latanya Sweeney and many others) have all proved this to be incorrect with many real world examples of taking so-called anonymous data and re-identifying individuals. With as little as 2 to 4 data points and a little understanding of programming, it's easy to crosscheck against other sources of data and reveal people's identity. As further proof, many companies purchase data for a specific purpose. An example of this would be a health research company. These research companies understand the issue of re-identifying individuals through data collection. For this very reason they are required to adhere to certain protocols which demand that they agree not to try and re-identify people. It's obvious that if they couldn't re-identify you from the data, they wouldn't need the provisions in place.[6]

This is a big deal and one for the reasons the FTC is rightly concerned about the data broker industry.

Myth #5: **Privacy is bad for business**

Those who use this retort believe privacy gets in the way of technology innovation. The opposite is in fact true. Privacy is totally compatible with business. While in the past, users were not as aware that they were giving away too much information, today increasing numbers are not happy at being tricked by the big data gatherers.

Online businesses, app developers, and others who want to succeed in the future will have to offer better options for users to control who has access to their data and how it's collected. Companies who put privacy first will do well, while those who abuse the trust of users will lose out.

Myth #6: **The privacy vs. security myth**

Benjamin Franklin is quoted as having said, "They who give up essential liberty to obtain a little temporary safety deserve neither liberty nor safety." You can quite easily exchange the terms liberty and safety for privacy and security. Both are desirable, both are necessary, and both are achievable. There is no need to give up privacy in order to be safe; likewise, we should never give up all our safety to remain private. A balance is required.

Those who spread this myth come from two extremes— overreach from governments that over time tend to lead towards dictatorships or anti-government extremists who don't trust anyone.

The fact is that most private citizens in a free society are supportive of reasonable safety and some surveillance, with oversight, from national security agencies. No one wants enemy spies or terrorists to be free to operate. But this should not be a tradeoff to having everyone in the country being spied on in order to track down the bad guys. National security should not mean that law-abiding citizens have to give up all their privacy. National security agencies should be able to quickly identity those they need to target. They should get warrants to track and have oversight to ensure they don't exceed clear boundaries. They should never simply suck up everyone's data just because they can and in case they want it later on. No one should sign up for that!

Myth #7: **Who would want to hack me?**

This myth is more of a misunderstanding. It's normally phrased like this: "I'm not famous, I'm not important or even that wealthy, so who would want to hack my computer?" Being famous, important, or wealthy are not qualifications that malware or hackers care about. If a malicious program infects your system, for example a ransomware attack, it's normally random. You just happened to (a) open the wrong attachment or (b) visited the wrong website. It has nothing to do with who you are.

If your email login or Internet banking details fall into the wrong hands, the hackers don't care who you are or how much money you may or may not have. They will use your account to send phishing emails or steal your funds just as they would from anyone else.

Additionally, the files on your laptop and phone are probably more important than you may realize. Your private information can enable identity theft, tax refund fraud, and other forms of fraud to be committed in your name. This type of crime happens every day to people just like you. That's reason enough to take cyber security and online privacy very seriously.

Myth #8: **I use anti-virus and a firewall so I'll be safe**

This is clearly a misunderstanding of cyber security and having too much confidence in certain security products.

First, there is no way any single product or service can ever keep you totally, 100% safe online. Security is like losing weight, you have to do lots of individual things right and making silly mistakes can blow your overall plan. However, by educating yourself and being pro-active you can minimize risks and boost protection.

Installing and keeping updated anti-malware (covers computer viruses and other attacks, is a good start, but it's only the very beginning. No anti-malware software gives a guarantee to catch all malware. (If you ever find one that does, don't believe it!) There are numerous other ways you can lose data. A semi-skilled hacker can steal from you even if you have a good firewall and anti-virus software installed.

Chapter 3:

Technologies That Make It All Possible

"As our technological powers increase, the side effects and potential hazards also escalate."
Alvin Toffler, Futurist, Technology author and writer

The simultaneous growth of several complementary technologies has provided the perfect storm for governments and business to collect and analyze data, and keep track of all of us. At the same time, Internet and mobile technologies are providing the perfect vector for cyber criminals to find and attack us.

The technologies that make this possible are: always on, high-speed Internet access; wearable small sensors; billions of mobile devices and cloud based big data analysis.

High-speed Internet—Online all the Time

According to Ernst & Young's Megatrends 2015 report, "broadband connections will rise from 2 billion today to almost 8 billion by 2019." Basically nearly all of humanity will be connected in some way.

It's no longer just teens and young adults who are spending their lives online. We are all "screenagers" now, hyper-connected using multi devices, online all the time.

It's reported that 84% of American adults use the Internet. With some demographic groups, such as younger adults,

Internet usage is already at full saturation point.[7] Even senior citizens, one of the least connected groups, are getting online in a big way with 58 % accessing and using the Internet.

In addition to the growth in the number of users, we are also all spending more time consuming digital media. In 2008, the average U.S. adult spent about 2.5 hours per day online. In 2015 this more than doubled to 5.6 hours per day online. The same growth trend can be seen worldwide as high-speed Internet continues to be deployed and smartphone growth continues.

Smart Sensors

Miniature smart sensors in wearable and mobile technology are prevalent in the fitness, health, consumer, sports, and entertainment device markets. Their widespread adoption is a key enabler in the growing Internet-of-Things ecosystem both in the home, in cars, and within the infrastructure in our malls and cities.

The cost of smart sensors has rapidly dropped. Also with advances in technology, these sensors have the ability to operate with less power consumption and with longer battery life. Therefore, smart sensors are being embedded into every kind of device and everywhere imaginable.

As James Bailey, Managing Director of mobility at technology consultancy group Accenture points outs, "The cost of sensors and devices is approaching free and the size is approaching invisible. Our perspective is literally everything will have IOT technology at some point."[8]

Smart sensors can collect real-time data and provide their feedback to mobile apps or gateway devices, which relay their readings to the Internet. As sensors grow ever cheaper, they will appear in more devices and in greater numbers, all generating more data that will be fed into larger cloud-based big datasets. According to the theory this will lead to more intelligent decisions in areas of design, product improvements, and delivery of services. Many of the benefits will be real. But the downside is that as more areas of our lives are recorded, without robust personal privacy rules in place, we will end up losing all sense of privacy.

Billions of Smartphones

While estimates vary, it's reported that anywhere from 65% to 80% of the world's population owns a mobile phone of some sort. As prices continue to drop, the majority will eventually switch from simple mobile phones to using smartphones. Mobile phone manufacturer Ericsson is forecasting 5.6 billion smartphone users by 2019.

The term "smartphone" is really a misnomer as they are essentially portable computing devices. A good illustration of this fact is that the average smartphone is used more for sending text messages, emails, playing games, and browsing the Internet than actually being used to make phone calls. According to a recent survey conducted by British Mobile Operator O2, calling is one of the least used features by many smartphone users.

In conjunction with the multiplication of smartphones, the number of available mobile apps for the devices has grown exponentially. According to Google, more than 75 billion Android apps were downloaded in 2014 and early 2015. However, many of these applications routinely abuse access to other parts of our phones. Some end up recording our phone calls and reading our messages and contact lists. Others send our location back to their developers. There are apps that look at our photos and steal our data. Most all of this activity is done without our knowledge.

With all the versatility of modern smartphones, it's no wonder they are often called the perfect spying device. Not only do we carry them everywhere we go, they provide numerous ways to remotely track us. Smartphones use a variety of methods to report our exact location plus they have cameras and sensitive microphones that can be operated remotely.

Big Data Analysis

Big data is big business. The ability to store and sort through huge silos of data has grown tremendously since 1997 when Michael Lesk published his research paper, "How Much Information is There in the World?" Lesk stated that by the year 2000, "we would be able to save everything—no information would be thrown away" and "there will be enough disk space and tape storage in the world to store everything people write, say, perform, or photograph."[9]

Fifteen years later, his foresight has proven to be totally accurate. According to research group IDC, everyone in the world created 2.8 zettabytes (ZB) (that's 2.8 trillion GBs) of data in 2012. This amount is doubling every year and a half. IDC forecasts we will generate 40 zettabytes by 2020.[10] There is actually so much big data being created and stored today that we are running out of ideas to describe it or put it into any context that makes sense to anyone other than a computer scientist.

The data comes from everywhere. Every minute of every day approximately 2.5 billion people are using the Internet.[11] Each minute millions of tweets, emails, and instant messages are sent. This also includes the constant countless postings to social media sites and forums and the production of digital videos and photos. All over the planet, smart sensors in cars, planes, alarm systems, connected household items, and medical devices are creating data that's recorded. Additionally e-commerce transaction records, credit card data, mobile phone geolocation coordinates, and dozens of other transactions and devices are producing new information that's collected and stored.

Even more impressive than the ability to simply store these huge amounts of structured and unstructured data, is the capability to connect the data dots and make new discoveries. The ability to search and analyze huge datasets can reveal valuable new insights hidden in the data.

Data analytics of big data is literally changing every field imaginable by uncovering new data relationships that were previously hidden. These new and sometimes unexpected patterns are helping business in all industries to solve complex problems and create new solutions.

However, these same techniques when applied to personal information quickly lead to loss of anonymity and privacy. Many privacy advocates are concerned with the way data brokers construct huge datasets of personal information in order to continually refine profiles.

Traditional privacy protection fails when personal data is collected and combined with additional data then the data is reused in additional ways that are not connected to the original collection. The combination of personal data collected from multiple sources when combined in big datasets quickly erodes personal anonymity. De-identification is the removal of personal identifying information from data. This is a useful tool, but it's far from perfect and is often badly practiced. Even when de-identification techniques are applied to the data, studies and real world examples have shown that because so much data is tied together, re-identification is still very possible.

Chapter 4:

Big Brother—We Are All Under Surveillance

"If the right to privacy means anything, it is the right of the individual, married or single, to be free from unwarranted governmental intrusion."
Justice William J. Brennan, Former United States Supreme Court Judge

"Relying on the government to protect your privacy is like asking a peeping tom to install your window blinds"
John Perry Barlow, founding member Electronic Frontier Foundation

I want to start off this section by stating I, as I believe most law-abiding citizens do, fully support the United States national intelligence agencies to do their jobs in protecting the citizens of the country. They, along with everyone in the Department of Defense, have a difficult job to perform and they fully deserve the support of the public.

However, there is a worrying worldwide trend concerning the increase in unrestricted government surveillance, which erodes the fundamental right of individual privacy. Along with the United States an increasing number of democratic countries such as Italy, Spain, Belgium, South Africa, Uganda, and others are deploying stealth citizen surveillance systems in secret. In other countries, like India, the population has even been advised that they do not have a right to privacy as a national ID system is deployed. While this kind of statement could be expected in repressive nations where individual freedoms are mostly restricted such as in China, much of the Middle East, North Korea, Cuba, etc., most European governments and the United States are involved in similar practices.

Drawing the line in balancing civil liberties with national defense and law enforcement is always going to be difficult. By nature we like to network and we need to be able to communicate freely without fear of intrusion from big brother surveillance programs. The problem with government surveillance programs is that they can be harmful just as easily as they can be used for our benefit. Government surveillance, as can be seen in numerous repressive countries, can easily be exploited as a powerful tool of censorship, coercion, political control, and repression. Surveillance of suspected jihadists, other terrorists, and drug lords is good; we all get that. But for regular citizens to have all their data sucked up or listened to by nameless, faceless strangers affects our behavior and limits our freedom of expression.

The Growth of the Surveillance State

Quis custodiet ipros custodes? (Translated "Who will watch the watchmen?")
Roman poet, Juvenal

Governments have always spied on their own citizens to some degree, although mostly only on those considered enemies of the state. However, since the horrific events of September 11, 2001 there has been a huge cultural shift in terms of how privacy, surveillance, and online security are viewed and deployed.

Worldwide governments are rapidly expanding online civilian surveillance capabilities. Citizen Lab, a Canadian technology and human rights research group, has detailed a growing number of national governments deploying not only mass cyber surveillance systems but also custom built spyware, mostly without informing their own citizens. The reasons are obvious—big brother government organizations around the world want to spy on their own people without restrictions.[12]

The attitude mostly exhibited by those in government who favor mass surveillance programs is that less individual privacy equals more security for everyone. Secrecy, a lack of technical understanding, and equivocal language in framing proposals are often contributing factors in gaining support from legislators for mass surveillance programs.

In 2013, Edward Snowden, the former NSA analyst turned whistle blower, made public his inside knowledge on numerous different government surveillance programs. He detailed what he saw as illegal bulk civilian surveillance programs being run by the U.S. government with intelligence shared with United Kingdom, Canadian, Australian, and New Zealand national intelligence agencies. To prove his case, Snowden turned over a huge cache of secret documents to journalists and fled the country. In return, the U.S. Department of Justice filed espionage charges against Snowden in 2013.

While Snowden has been vilified by the intelligence community and the administration, a huge percentage of the population, including some members of Congress and the House of Representatives, have been appalled by the scope of the unsupervised NSA surveillance overreach he helped expose. As a result, several pieces of legislation have been introduced to try and curb the wholesale collection of records without judicial approval.

There is no denying the fact that we now live in a very dangerous world. Terrorist groups like ISIS and Al Qaeda are increasingly using jihadist hackers to recruit more followers, to target and attack Western businesses and infrastructure.[13] It would be foolish not to expect national intelligence agencies to try and track down militant Islamic radicals residing in the West. This is especially relevant if these radicals are aiding terror groups or being groomed as extremists. Much of this surveillance can be conducted online. On the other hand, the problem is that we all get caught up in broad cyber dragnets aimed at radicals and lose our privacy in the name of overall national security. While some surveillance is necessary in providing protection, it needs to be deployed with restraint and oversight, especially when used against citizens who have done nothing illegal.

Secret Programs

The NSA and other national intelligence agencies all run secret programs, and they want to keep them secret for a reason. We also know that national intelligence agencies have lied and will lie to Congress about their activities. So why should we expect anything else and believe them now? When Senator Ron Wyden D-Oregon, asked in 2013 whether the government was collecting data on millions of Americans, Director of National Intelligence James Clapper said no. We now know that was not true.

As William Binney, former high-level NSA code breaker, who spent 30 years at the NSA says, "The NSA lies about what it stores. At least 80% of fiber-optic cables globally go via the U.S. This is no accident and allows the U.S. to view all communication coming in. At least 80% of all audio calls, not just metadata, are recorded and stored in the U.S."[14]

The unfortunate fact is the more connected our lives become, the more data we are giving away and big brother agencies will find a way to gather whatever data they want. They will continue to run secret programs. In many cases, just because they can, and in their minds, just in case they need it later.

In addition to bulk online surveillance, a proxy war of cyber espionage and warfare is being played out. As a civilian it's easy to get caught up if you work in any targeted industry.

By and large the USA doesn't seem to spy on foreign companies to steal their technology for profit. Unlike many other nation states actively involved with large scale cyber warfare and surveillance programs, the United States doesn't seem to be involved with cyber espionage for financial and commercial gain. Its efforts, as far as can be assessed, are targeted toward tracking enemies of the state, or those that could become enemies.

The same can't be said for the majority of Chinese state sponsored hacking of U.S., Canadian, and other Western businesses. There have been way too many cases of data breaches linked directly back to Chinese (presumably military) hackers. They blatantly steal engineering plans and trade secrets in almost every area of technology, military, healthcare, and other hi-tech industries . [15] , [16] In May 2014, the Department of Justice charged five officials in the Chinese military with hacking into U.S. private sector companies to pilfer sensitive business information. [17]

A recent development is that of foreign governments launching cyber sabotage strikes against companies or individuals that are critical of them, as happened in the case of the North Korean hacker attacks on Sony Pictures. They destroyed Sony company data, stole unreleased movies, put them online, and published company emails. Likewise in February 2014, the Las Vegas Sands casino group was attacked by Iranian government hackers. This was in retaliation for comments made against that country by the chief executive officer and majority owner, billionaire Sheldon Adelson. His comments in late 2013 had caused the Iranian leadership to vow revenge. The attack was just that and wiped data off thousands of servers and IT systems causing significant damage. [18]

The War Over Encryption

In the name of national security there are calls for restricting, weakening, or outright banning encryption technologies.[19] This is happening in numerous countries. While no one denies that some hackers and thieves use encryption, but so do those who are persecuted by repressive governments. The United Nations Office of the High Commissioner for Human Rights released a report in June 2015 confirming the useful role of encryption and anonymity on the Internet. They concluded that these technologies protect individuals by allowing them to exercise their right to freedom of opinion and expression and deserve strong protection.[20]

It has been well documented how the FBI (and the British government) tried to put pressure on Microsoft to build backdoors into the BitLocker encryption program. (BitLocker is the default file encryption product that is part of Windows.) Microsoft engineers involved with the project have publicly stated they have not complied with these requests.

One company however that has agreed to work with Federal agencies is Research in Motion, the makers of BlackBerry phones. They recently told delegates at an IT summit that they will work with law enforcement to allow access to their devices in effect building a backdoor and giving the key to federal agencies. [21]

Weakening or outright banning encryption is a very real threat to online security and privacy for everyone. Without strong encryption technology, you can't have secure online security, secure online banking, or any form of secure online commerce. Building backdoors into encryption products is just as bad and makes us all less safe.

Whenever you build a backdoor into a product there is nothing to stop malicious hackers from finding and using them as well. Hackers won't stop looking if they know there are hidden backdoors in encryption products and eventually they will find and exploit them. Thus you weaken everyone's security.

In a predictable response to the numerous privacy solutions being developed since the Edward Snowden event, law enforcement has been quick to once again target and demonize the use of encryption. In late 2014, Apple and Google both announced they would add default mobile phone encryption. This could only be opened by the customer and not by the technology companies themselves (iPhone 6 and new Android phones from October 2014.) [22] The FBI quickly spoke out against this.[23], [24] However, rather than crying wolf, a better outcome would have been for FBI director James Comey to agree to a conditional encryption. The condition would be that with a warrant they could still force anyone to hand over the encryption keys to their phone or risk going to jail. In fact, the Supreme Court had already told the FBI the same thing (Riley v. California) to get a warrant if they want to search cellphones.[25]

Chief Justice John G. Roberts Jr. wrote, "The fact that technology now allows an individual to carry such information in his hand does not make the information any less worthy of the protection for which the Founders fought."

But this has not stopped FBI Director James Comey from continuing to put forward his case to stop default encryption technology at every turn.[26] The debate is ongoing. At the time of writing this book both the Senate Judiciary Committee and the Senate Intelligence Committee are holding hearings on strong encryption, privacy, and what the FBI terms as the threat of "Going Dark."

The issue no one has addressed yet is how US law enforcement agencies think they can force foreign companies into building backdoors in their encryption products. The answer is they can't. So if US technology companies are forced to comply, this will simply force those who want encryption to use products developed beyond the reach of the US legal system.

How this will affect all of us remains to be seen. In the meanwhile, it makes perfect sense to use encryption to protect your data and communications from snoops, hackers, and anyone else who has no business looking at your private data. Of course, that won't always stop national intelligence agencies from spying on you if they feel you warrant it.

National Intelligence Agencies Spying on You

The majority of intelligence agencies and military departments that write malware use it to gather intelligence. As data has moved from written records to digital data, spying has likewise moved into the realm of computer hacking and targeted malware attacks to gather information.

Specially written spyware is used by law enforcement in numerous countries to infect the computers and devices of those suspected of crimes. Malware is used as an investigative tool by law enforcement. As more people use encryption to access the Internet and to secure their communications, the only way law enforcement can see what suspects are doing is to infect their computer. Systems become infected with targeted malware like key-loggers that record passwords and allow access system resources like cameras and microphones, which can be operated remotely if necessary.

Groups like Hacking Team from Italy create malware for governments to spy on their citizens. These "digital mercenaries" and others like them use unreported flaws in browsers, plug-ins like Flash and Java, and other common programs to install their spyware on victim's devices. In many cases they create the programs and provide them to foreign governments who use them to access digital phones, tablets, and computers of their citizens, basically classic big-brother spying.[27]

Big Brother Summation

The NSA is probably the best funded and most technically competent national intelligence agency in the world.

They are tasked with a difficult job of being protectors of the digital front line in an ever-changing proxy war. However, many cyber security experts including ex-NSA members agree there is a huge overreach and lack of oversight to their activities.

State sponsored mass surveillance is not going to decrease anytime soon, if ever. So if you want to keep your life and secrets private, don't put everything in a digital format and be prepared to choose security over convenience. Low-tech pen and paper can't be hacked remotely!

Chapter 5:

Business—We Are The Product

"Addressing the privacy challenges of big data is first and foremost the responsibility of those collecting and using consumer information. The time has come for businesses to move their data collection and use practices out of the shadows and into the sunlight."
Edith Ramirez, FTC chairwoman

While governments want to track, control, and censor their citizens, commercial businesses are all about collecting, tracking, and selling your private data to advertisers and data brokers. Additionally, businesses use data collected for research, analytical purposes, and to improve their product and service offerings. Business marketers will tell us they are doing us all a favor by profiling us, that they only have our best interests at heart when they use the data they have collected on us to try and influence our behavior.

Businesses have been collecting their customer's personal information for years. That's a normal and acceptable business practice. However, as technology has increased, the ease with which to track and bulk collect, store, and analyze customer data has gone into overdrive. Understanding your customer is vital for businesses to improve their products and services. However, just as when dealing with government surveillance, business surveillance, tracking and bulk data collection, can easily become creepy. Even if the intention is only to influence buying behavior and/or improve business offerings. Privacy regulations and legislation are playing catch up in most industries.

Online and offline data brokers have built huge data warehouses filled with personally identifiable information profiles for each one of us. They collect all our location data; they know our likes, interests, browsing history, full demographics, and more. For many years the pendulum has swung into the area where businesses have an "anything goes" attitude towards collecting user's data with data broker firms being the major culprit for overreaching in this area.

As far as most big businesses are concerned, they assume that we (consumers, customers, users of their products, etc.) don't really care about our personal privacy or anonymity. They have been collecting data that we have self-contributed for years. So if we are giving our data away, big business reasonably assumes we don't value it and we don't mind if they collect it. Of course, if you actually explain to most people that they are under surveillance by the very companies who have sold them their technology and whose websites and services they use online, most are actually very concerned. In many cases they are annoyed and feel they have been duped for having given away so much personal, private information.

In validation of this, in a recent Pew study (2015) as many as 90% of those surveyed were concerned about the invasion of their privacy by businesses over-collecting personal identifiable data. Plus in a surprising report published by USA Network, 55% of young people said they would like to get rid of social media if there was a way to erase all of the personal data they have already over-shared. In the same study, up to 75% would think of deactivating their accounts if privacy breaches continued.[28] My bet is if they really knew how much data was being collected and what it was being used for, they would feel even more strongly about the issue.

Even some technology leaders are now realizing that the loss of privacy is bad for their business. Tim Cook, Apple CEO, has been outspoken recently regarding this very subject. At an Electronic Privacy Information Center event in Washington DC, he put it this way, "We don't think you should ever have to trade it (your personal information) for a service you think is free but actually comes at a very high cost . . . prominent and successful companies have built their businesses by lulling their customers into complacency about their personal information." Those "prominent and successful companies" being Facebook, LinkedIn, Google, Yahoo, Instagram, and the host of other social media businesses, which feed off their users' information in exchange for their "free service." There is no free lunch is a lesson many of today's netizens - Internet citizens – have yet to learn.

Technology Consumers are the Product

The software and online industries have all changed their business models in the last 15 years. Pre-2000, you were a customer who purchased a license to use software or an online service. Post the dotcom crash of 2000, many Internet companies changed their business models from selling products to selling customer information. When Facebook launched its social media platform, consumers rushed to sign up for the "free service," paying by giving away their personal information. Many other vendors followed the same business model. Give away a product, sign up lots of users, harvest and sell their personal information. Today, selling personal information is a second revenue stream for multiple companies.

Fortunately there is a ray of light at the end of the tunnel. Some technology firms are getting the message that not everyone is happy with all their personal information being collected and sold. At the February 2015 Summit on Cyber Security and Consumer protection, Tim Cook, Apple's CEO, repeatedly focused on the importance of privacy in his speech: "If those of us in positions of responsibility fail to do everything in our power to protect the right of privacy, we risk something far more valuable than money. We risk our way of life." Cook also stated that Apple's business model was focused on providing products and services, not on selling their customers' personal data. Cook's comments are a move in the right direction, which will hopefully grow. In the meantime, it's up to consumers to protect themselves as best as they can.

Terms of Service—Complex by Design

The terms of service, the legal agreements and privacy policies we all "accept," are part of the problem. Most websites, social media sites, and other online web services present their users with long, hard to read and comprehend legal agreements before they can download or access a service. It's a total sham. They are overly complex by design.

Whenever you download an app or register to use an online service, you are required to check a box stating you agree with the terms of service. Everyone does this, mostly without reading what you have just agreed to. When did you last read every detail and the small print before checking the box? The small print details the use of the service and covers the privacy policy. And this is where we are all agreeing to give our data away. Online companies who collect users' data are fully aware that most Internet users don't fully understand how and what data is being collected about them or how it will be used.[29]

Privacy policies and terms of use are long and written in a way that discourages users from reading them. These agreements are usually only written for one audience and that's not your typical end-users. They are written by lawyers for lawyers. In other words, the language used is written to be as complex as possible. Most regular consumers don't read them because they are long, boring, and complex by design.

The simple fact is even if you want to read the terms of service for every website and forum you use it wouldn't be possible. According to research conducted at Carnegie Mellon University, it would take the average web user approximately 250 hours, which translates to more than a full working month (every year) just to read the actual privacy policies for the websites they visit and the services they use.[30]

56

In addition to overall complex agreements, there are numerous other data issues with big business data collection that should concern us all.

The Anonymity Problem

When a business collects and stores personal data from their customers, there is a growing body of legislation they need to comply with. In order to share the data collected with their business partners or to sell it, they must de-identity individual data so as to preserve the anonymity of the individual. This approach is highly problematic. There is no standard definition for de-identifying data. Each state has its own standard as does each industry. Plus as more types of data are collected from an ever-increasing range of connected devices, any current definition will quickly become outdated. For example, if a car manufacturer collects location data, note how difficult it is to anonymize. The data is easily cross-referenced with data from numerous other agencies and companies. It's not difficult to re-identify who owns the vehicle, where they live, and where they go.

TRUSTe defines PII (Personally Identifiable Information) as "any information or combination of information that can be used to identify, contact, or locate a discrete individual." This defines the problem with so much data being collected. Nearly ALL data collected about or from an individual can be turned into PII when it's combined with other data, thus making true anonymity difficult to achieve.

By linking de-identified data to other identifiers (IP address—a machine readable, numeric Internet address, email, geo-location data, tracking cookies, device fingerprint, age, gender, ethnic grouping, place of employment, zip code, handwriting analysis, etc.), it's still possible to re-identify most individuals with as little as 2 to 4 data points. This is a major problem to anyone who wants to remain anonymous.

Truly anonymous data that cannot be linked to an individual is hard to achieve and it's even more difficult with the more data you have. Data scientists have for many years argued that anonymity of PII is almost impossible as all data is personal when combined with enough other related data.[31] The so-called Netflix case illustrates this point. Anonymous data from Netflix was paired with movie recommendations from the Internet Movie Database website (Imbd.com). This allowed the researchers to easily identify individuals from the "anonymous" data that Netflix had provided. So what is considered "personal" information is an ever-growing category and could now include random information like movie rentals and reviews!

The Security Problem

The other really disappointing news about corporations collecting all our personal data is they have proven how inept many of them are at keeping it safe. Uber, eBay, Adobe, LinkedIn, TJ Maxx, Target, Home Depot, Anthem Insurance, Municipal Bond Insurance Association, and numerous other companies have exposed and leaked personal data by their businesses being compromised. Customers of these companies are left vulnerable and exposed often without realizing it.

Almost every week there is another story about how a large, once trusted entity has been hacked, lost data, or exposed confidential customer data through a misconfigured server, a phishing attack, a disgruntled employee, or some other form of data breach.

Some recent examples:

- Between April and June of 2014, Community Health Systems, a major U.S. hospital chain, was hacked by Chinese attackers.[32] The 4.5 million records taken included names, addresses, phone numbers, birthdates, and social security numbers. In other words, everything a hacker would require for identity theft and fraud.

- In August 2014, a service agent at Cox Communications was socially engineered (tricked) into giving account login details to a caller claiming to be a technical support staff member. This allowed the fraudulent caller to access internal customer records including names, addresses, emails, account PINS, secret account questions, and the last four digits of social security or driver license numbers.[33]

- In August 2014, an administrator server error was discovered at E.A. Conway Medical Center (part of University Health Center) that leaked data to the open Internet. Prof. Sam Bowne at City College San Francisco came across an open FTP server full of medical records simply by conducting a Google search. The information that was available to anyone who looked included names, account numbers, payment amounts, and addresses for 6,073 accounts.[34]

- In early October 2014, the Municipal Bond Insurance Association (MBIA), the largest bond insurer in the United States, exposed information including bank accounts and routing numbers, balances, dividends, and account names via a badly configured Oracle Reports database server. Normally, this type of information would only be accessible to an internal, authorized user. However, the misconfigured database exposed this highly confidential banking data, with access to hundreds of millions of dollars in tax-payer funds. This financial data was made accessible on the Internet and via Google search.[35] While MBIA works with corporate clients, the same errors occur with companies handling personal individual information.

- The University of Maryland,[36] Auburn University,[37] North Dakota University, Butler University, and Indiana

University all exposed the private information or had serious data breaches resulting in hundreds of thousands of student records being stolen in 2014 and early 2015.

It's very clear from these and literally hundreds of other similar cases that corporate companies do not have a good track record when it comes to protecting your personally identifiable information. As mentioned elsewhere in this book, at the time of writing (October 2015) there were 450 cases listed by the Identity Theft Resource Center in the USA, where over 135 million data records of personal information were either stolen or exposed.

While some hacks are discovered fairly quickly, most are not. According to many in the cyber security field, most businesses should assume that hackers have been able to infect their networks and get into their servers. This may sound far-fetched and even scary to a non-IT professional, but today it's standard for business IT security teams to assume their organization has already been compromised. Anti-malware products literally can't keep up with new malware attacks, and most companies and government departments are constantly playing catch-up in patching their systems. Additionally, as employees continue to use personal devices to access company systems, it is not difficult for determined attackers to find a way to get inside company defenses. Even when a company does discover a breach, many businesses do not have anti-exfiltration technology in place that would stop hackers from extracting information from the company. It often takes them some time to find and close the doors to data theft.

Lastly, after a business learns it has lost information, it can take upwards of 30 days to start the process of informing its customers, partners, and employees. Each state has its own data breach notification legislation, which businesses have to comply with. Some states have stricter laws than others. Although a Federal breach law to inform when data has been exposed is being debated, nothing has been finalized yet. In any case, by the time the public hears their information has been stolen, the data is long gone and has already been disseminated across the cyber criminal black market.

In summary, the public in general is far too trusting and free with giving their information to companies that simply don't have their act together. In many cases, there is simply nothing you can do to stop your data being taken. Thus it's imperative that you are diligent to take steps to stop any criminals from using data they may have already stolen.

Data Brokers Inc.

Data brokers are like the shady middlemen of the modern information economy. They are public data aggregators who collect, store, and sell data on almost every aspect of American consumer's lives. They treat personal data as a commodity. They collect and buy data from everyone and sell to anyone who will pay them with few restrictions.

The Data Broker Industry

Your personal data is worth a lot of money. The only problem is you are not getting paid for it! It's simply being taken from you and sold, often without your knowledge or consent. The profit made from collecting, sorting, and selling personal data runs into billions of dollars.

There are thousands of commercial data gathering companies involved in collecting, sorting, and selling your personal data. As an industry, data brokers are one of the greatest threats to everyone's personal privacy. Many of these companies call themselves by other names including information brokers, data marketing brokers, or information list brokers. That's simply a way of putting lipstick on the pig, as they try to appear more legitimate. They treat personal data as a commodity and buy and sell to each other and other commercial entities without informing anyone.

Whatever they call themselves, they all make money collecting, recycling, sorting, and selling data created by and/or about private individuals. Much of this business is not illegal, but it's certainly shady and mostly hidden from the public. You visit a website, they record that. You click on a link, and they got that too. You watch an online video, and they want a piece of that as well. Offline, you visit a store and make a purchase. The data broker vultures want that information as well. What you purchased, where you went, how you paid, all the details are added to a big data system to be included in your profile. Like a multi-tentacled octopus, data brokering firms have got their hooks into almost every aspect of your life. They don't care if you care or not, as long as they can make a buck out of tracking you.

This multi-million dollar industry resides firmly in a troubling grey area. While technically legal, a growing number of people (the author included) feel that the data brokering industry is highly unethical in its business practices. While there are legitimate reasons for companies to run background checks on individuals and businesses, the amount of data that's collected goes way beyond what is necessary to make qualified business decisions.

It's not only the amount of information that data brokers are sucking up that is concerning, it's the stealth methods that they employ. Most consumers are naïve and have little understanding that almost every time they complete a survey, make a purchase, or sign up for a new service, the information is collected and sold. Likewise, when posting personal data on the Internet, it gets collected by some data broker.

Thus data brokers know almost everything about the U.S. adult population. They know who is pregnant or trying to lose weight. They know who's single, married, or divorced. For a fee, they can provide details about you to anyone who wants to know. Information such as: if you smoke; what your religious views are; the type of car you drive (and what you paid for it);

where you work; live, and shop. Their aggressive collection of personal data is almost invasive and comes as a shock to most people. There is almost no area that is off limits for data brokers when it comes to collecting personal data. Likewise, there is almost no company they won't sell your personal data to.

One of the big lies that data brokers continually push is that the data they sell is mostly anonymous. That's simply not true. It's been proven many times that by intersecting datasets, anyone with some skill can quickly de-anonymize ordinary people, compromising their privacy. As previously discussed, we know that with just a few data points, identities can be uncovered. This seems to be of little concern to data brokers. Their focus is solely on making money.

The sprawling data broker industry is comprised of several thousand companies that collect, segment. and sell our personal data in some way. The industry is complex with multiple layers of data brokers (many are specialized), collecting data from different data sources. They buy and sell to each other and other commercial entities without informing anyone. They all sell to each other and trade to build bigger, more complete profiles of information on each of us. All data brokers fit into one of three broad categories.

- **Direct Marketing Data Brokers:** These companies have built enormous data profiles on every one of us in order to market products. Some of the largest have up to 1,500 individual data points of information on everyone in their big data systems. They know everything about your habits and lifestyle. And they supply this information to marketers and advertisers so they can target and hopefully sell all of us more stuff. To justify their business model, direct marketing data brokers use the tag line, "without us you wouldn't receive relevant offerings." We need to know that this is nonsense! What data brokers should say is that without them, we wouldn't receive so much pointless junk mail and we wouldn't have to worry so much about identity theft. (The credit rating bureaus are data brokers as well, just with more legislation.) If anyone wants to find a product, we all know how to use search engines and where the stores are. For our special interests, we follow blogs, or read magazines, articles, and books. Most data brokers that supply marketers simply add to the huge amounts of spam and junk mail we all receive, both online and in our physical mailboxes.

- **Risk Mitigation Services:** those involved in risk mitigation. These are all involved in identity verification and fraud detection. The credit rating agencies fall into this category and are the only data brokers who are currently regulated sufficiently.

- **People Finder Services:** Lastly, there are data brokers who focus on people search. These are the companies that allow anyone to look you up online. In my opinion, they are the most dangerous of all. If an identity thief wants to impersonate you, this is where they can go to get information on you. People search data brokers can also be used by stalkers, snoops, or anyone else who wants to find you. We all know that the Internet can be offensive at times and people will say things online that they wouldn't to your face. As mentioned in the introduction, there are many people who don't want to be found. Not because they have done anything illegal, but because they are concerned for their privacy and in many cases for the safety of themselves and their families. If the Pew Research figures from October 2014 are correct, then 40% of users have been subjected to online harassment, intimidation, and bullying of some kind.[38] Online harassment can go all the way from simply name calling, to stalking, to threats of physical violence and death.

Doxxing as a form of harassment is another growing problem. This is posting another person's private information online including their home address, contact details, and even financial data with the aim of encouraging physical intimidation or harm. Data broker and people finder sites enable doxxing by providing personal details online to anyone who cares to search for them. While some social media sites like Twitter have banned doxxing, there are many other forums and online platforms that don't.

In addition there are lots of people who shouldn't be listed in people search websites. The list would include:

- Those in law enforcement and their families.

- Those in the military and their families.
  - Already we have seen terrorist groups like ISIS actively using social media to target the families of soldiers. Although there is no evidence, I wouldn't be at all surprised to find they use people finder data broker services to track down military families. There is certainly nothing to stop them from doing so.

- Those in the media. Without a free press, freedom cannot survive. Journalists shouldn't have to be concerned that their private information is available online, which would make them more vulnerable to intimidation for reporting the truth.

- Those who have been victims of abuse or a crime.

- Incident victims who have to testify in lawsuits.

- Victims of identity theft or other kinds of fraud.

- Those afraid of ex-spouses or partners.

- Politicians or other political figures.

- Celebrities and high-profile sports figures concerned for their privacy.

There are so many problems with data brokers. We will look at a few of them here including (a) security concerns, (b) data accuracy concerns, and (c) Federal regulatory concerns

Security Concerns

"There are two kinds of businesses. Those that have been hacked and those that don't know they've been hacked."
FBI Director James Comey

There is no such thing as a totally secure network. Anyone or any company that claims otherwise is ill informed. Cyber criminals know data brokering firms are goldmines of information. Personally identifiable information is worth a lot of money on the cyber underground. Here it can be sold to enable identity fraud, identity theft, and to gain access to other systems. The vast treasure troves of data collected by the data brokering industry are huge targets for skilled cyber criminals.

With data brokers sucking up millions of data points of personally identifiable information and storing it, there are legitimate concerns about how safe they actually keep our information. When questioned, data brokering firms all make ambiguous references to encryption and IT security best practices. They also tell us that they go to great lengths to protect personally identifiable information. However, in theory, their guarantees of protecting the information they trade are mostly useless. As any experienced cyber security professional will tell you, there is no such thing as a totally secure system, especially one that is open to the Internet.

As renowned security researcher Bruce Schneier says, "With few exceptions, our secrets are stored on computers and networks vulnerable to hacking. It's much easier to break into networks than it is to secure them, and large organizational networks are very complicated and full of security holes. Bottom line: If someone sufficiently skilled, funded, and motivated wants to steal an organization's secrets, they will succeed."[39]

All IT systems have unpatched applications and in nearly all cases undiscovered vulnerabilities. It's not that companies don't want to be secure and don't do their best to find and patch all their systems. It's just a fact, you can have 500 servers and if 499 are patched, that last server is leaving a wide-open hole that a hacker can exploit. Then there are the dozens of different applications and computer security products that are found in all organizations. The simple truth is not all of them will be deployed and configured correctly to provide total security.

Many high-profile celebs have had their personal information stolen from hacked data broker sites and sold online: Bill Gates, Michelle Obama, Beyoncé, Jay-Z , Ashton

Kutcher, former FBI Director Robert Mueller, and many others.[40]

With several high-profile hacks on their systems, the data brokering industry doesn't have a good security record with most of the largest companies having being hacked. Both LexisNexis[41] and Dun & Bradstreet,[42] two of the giants in the industry had their systems breached. The intrepid attackers then installed backdoors, which allowed them to siphon off data records at will. They then set up their own online website and proceeded to sell the stolen data on the criminal underground. Information leaked included Social Security numbers, birthdates, driver license records, and enough other personal information useful to commit identity theft, fraud, and other financial crimes against the victims. There is no doubt that more will be breached in the future.

Sometimes, it's not even necessary to hack into a company to get information. Hieu Minh Ngo, a Vietnamese national managed to fool data brokering firm Court Ventures, now part of Experian,[43] that he was a U.S. based private investigator. Between 2007 and early 2013, Court sold personal private information on approximately 200 million U.S. adults to Ngo. This included names, date of birth, Social Security numbers, bank account details and routing numbers, credit card numbers, expiration dates, CVV numbers, and addresses and phone numbers. In other words, everything required to commit identity theft and fraud. Ngo used this information to set up an online marketplace where he sold the fraudulently acquired information to would-be identity thieves and other online criminals. When the U.S. Secret Service finally captured Ngo, details in his guilty plea and subsequent investigations revealed the extent of the damage done.

According to the Internal Revenue Service (IRS), well over 13,000 U.S. citizens were victims of $65 million in fraudulent individual income tax return fraud. These were all filed with personal information that Ngo had sold to ID thieves, information supplied by Court Services and Experian. The amount of credit card and other fraud committed with information sold by Ngo may never be known, however it's probably in the many millions of U.S. dollars. Ngo is now serving a well deserved 13-year prison sentence, having been found guilty of wire fraud, identity theft, access device fraud, and four counts of computer fraud and abuse.[44]

The Ngo case highlights the lack of due diligence conducted by both Court Ventures and Experian, and the subsequent denial by Experian that any real damage had taken place. This is a confirmation of the indifferent attitude that data brokers have toward us, the public whose personal data is simply merchandise to them.[45]

Then there is the reporting problem once a data breach/ information theft takes place. On average it takes over 200 days, sometimes it's a year or more, before a data breach is discovered. Add to this the months before the average company reports the break-in and data theft. This means any hacker has, in most cases months, years to act and exploit any personal data they can extract from a data broker's store of information. The balance of power is also shifting towards the attackers, with more data brokers holding increasing amounts of personal data. So the attackers target is growing in size, and the likelihood of your personal data being stolen is an ever-increasing risk.

Accuracy Problems

An additional issue with data brokers collecting huge amounts of personal data is the fact that there is currently no method for checking the accuracy of the data. Accuracy is not so vital if you are being sent marketing mailers (junk mail). However, it becomes a considerable problem if inaccurate information is being used for background checks for employment, insurance, and other services. Inaccurate information makes a big difference to the average person who would have no idea what data records were checked and no way to correct any inconsistencies.

Journalists who have researched this issue and checked their own files (sometimes not very easy to do at all), have found mixed results. Some data broker's data is scary accurate, showing for example every address a person has ever lived at, all the phone numbers they have ever had, lists of all neighbors at every address, etc. Yet records held by other data brokers have been totally inaccurate and contain lots of weird data. This could be the result of people with the same or similar names just getting mixed up, or it could be errors were made while collecting the data. Either way the results can be difficult to correct and take a long time. (As anyone who has had to clean up credit records after identity theft will confirm.)

Take for example the case of Alexandria Goree from St. Louis. She sued the big three credit rating companies, Experian, TransUnion, and Equifax over inaccurate information they had in her file. Sometime in 2013, a credit reported showed she was deceased. Even after months of trying to prove to the three companies that she was very much alive, they didn't remove the deceased notation. The result was not only frustrating, but also made her life very difficult. During this period she was unable to get any new credit and was turned down numerous times while trying to find a place to live.[46]

Goree's is not an isolated case either. According to an FTC report from December 2012, one in four consumers find mistakes in their credit files.[47] While the credit reporting companies are regulated and consumers have simple access to check their reports, the data held in the thousands of data broker's files is not anywhere nearly as accessible. It's reasonable to assume that the error rate is about the same. If that's the case, there are millions of incorrect data records and millions of decisions made in background checks based on faulty data held in data broker files. It's time the FTC regulated data brokers and stopped the wholesale collection of everyone's data, unless it's by opt-in with the chance for consumers to verify.

For some time, Federal regulators have been concerned about the amount of personal data that the data brokering industry has been amassing. Yet underfunded regulators are simply not able to keep up with the mass of firms gorging themselves on consumer's personal data.

Plus in the future with Internet-of-Things and hundreds of household devices all connected to the Internet, the result will be an even bigger tidal wave of personal data being collected, stored, analyzed, and sold. We can predict that the trade of personally identifiable data will continue to increase. Unless the FTC or other regulators steps in, the future will have an almost complete lack of privacy.

Data Brokers: Action Steps

- Opt out of the largest data broker sites. If you have the time and it's important enough to you, make opting out of data brokers an ongoing exercise. The challenge is that even though you may get your data removed from being displayed in public searches, if you move or change services (Internet service providers, phone or other services) or sign up for a new subscription, a new set of data brokers may re-acquire your data and include it all over again.

While there are thousands of data brokers, these are some of the biggest to contact and opt out (links below). Note most data brokers will make it as difficult as possible to opt out. Many require you fax your data opt out request to them.

- **Spokeo** http://www.spokeo.com/opt_out/new

- **Pipl** https://pipl.com/directory/remove/

- **ZoomInfo**
  http://www.zoominfo.com/lookupEmail

- **Whitepages**
  https://support.whitepages.com/hc/en-us/articles/203263794-How-do-I-remove-my-people-search-profile-

- **PeopleSmart**
  https://www.peoplesmart.com/optout-go

- **CheckPeople**
  http://www.checkpeople.com/optout

- **BeenVerified**
  http://www.beenverified.com/optout

- **Intelius** https://www.intelius.com/optout.php

- **PublicRecords360** have an online opt out form, but it's a Google Docs form, which means if you use the online form, then Google will have all your data as well. Better to fax your data request (425-974-6194) or email it to them (optout@publicrecords360.com)

- **ZabaSearch**

In addition to opting out of the data broker sites listed above, the following actions will help you to keep your personal information and details from being collected.

- Pay cash in retail stores. Data brokers collect information on what you pay for with debit and credit cards. This can cause problems. For instance, buying certain allergy medications can get you labeled as an allergy sufferer and added to your profile as such. If you need to use your cards, at least game their system. Buy health goods at higher end stores, this will give you the benefit of not being labeled unhealthy or financially challenged! Paying cash stops the collection of your purchase data as there is no paper trail.

- Don't complete warranty cards. This data almost always ends up with data brokers. Your warranty is still valid as long as you have the proof-of-purchase. The only thing a warranty card does is get you added into a marketing database.

- Limit free apps on all your mobile devices. You pay for them with your data, which often ends up in a data broker's system.

Chapter 6

Cyber Crime—The Curse of the Information Age

"It's disturbingly easy to become a hacker millionaire."
Security company, Trustwave

"The criminal hacker mindset doesn't actually see what happens on the other side, to the victims."
Kevin Mitnick, security consultant and formally the FBI's most wanted criminal hacker

We Have Your Files, Now Pay Up

* Based on a true story, names changed to protect the privacy of those involved.

Paul, who lives in Los Angeles, was roused from sleep early one Monday morning by his sister, Sarah, calling from Boston. "My computer is locked," she explained, "and I have a note from the FBI saying I have to pay a fine in Bitcoins. What do I do?" Paul worked in IT, so it was natural for his sister to call him, but this was not a normal technical request. Sarah's computer had been attacked by ransomware and all her business and personal files had been locked (encrypted). The "FBI" notice was bogus. It had been created by miscreants in Eastern Europe to make their demand for a cash "ransom payment" look more authentic.

Paul knew the drill, he had read about CryptoWall and other "ransomware" malware. He knew if Sarah didn't pay up, the initial fee of $500 would double. If she still didn't pay in the time requested, her files would be gone forever. This would be disastrous for her small business.

Paul assured his sister that he could help her and that this wasn't the actual FBI locking her system. It was malicious cyber criminals who had fooled her into clicking or opening an attachment that led to her system being infected. "But Paul, is there another way, without paying these creeps $500? And what are Bitcoins anyway? I need my files, Paul, please help me get them back." Paul explained, "No, sorry Sarah, there is no other way to get your files back unless you have complete, up-to-date back ups of all your work." Paul already knew the answer to that, he was always telling his family and friends to back up, to upgrade their software, to not click on links in emails, but he knew most didn't follow his advice. The only thing for Sarah to do was to make a cash deposit via her bank to the unique Bitcoin wallet the ransomers had provided. Much as she hated the idea of paying out $500, Sarah followed the instructions given. Despite being very concerned that she was "throwing" money away, the criminals kept their side of the one-sided deal and sent the encryption key allowing her to retrieve all of her files.

Today Sarah makes regular backups. She also runs the latest anti-malware software and is very careful never to open attachments or click on links in emails. Paul uses her story to encourage his clients, colleagues, and friends to take cyber crime precautions seriously.

The Growing Cyber Crime Wave

That there is a growing cyber crime wave shouldn't really be news to anyone. It's estimated that over 500 million victims are impacted annually at a rate of around 18 every second worldwide. [48]

The old saying that "crime doesn't pay" simply doesn't apply to cyber crime. Cyber crime is not only prolific, it is also very profitable for many. It's a worldwide problem that continues to grow and is being driven by increasingly well-organized groups, both criminal and political.[49] Look into any part of the Internet and at almost any technology and you will find hackers at work, waiting to deceive, trick, and exploit to infect systems and steal data. In the last year alone literally hundreds of millions of emails, login details, credit cards numbers, and other records of personally identifiable information have been stolen by criminal hackers. This trend is not only continuing but is accelerating.

A Brief History of Computer Crime

The motivation behind nearly all malicious hacking and cyber crime is ultimately money. And the profits make it worthwhile for most criminals. However, it wasn't always like this. Since the first computer viruses appeared in the mid-1980s, there has been a steady stream of viruses, worms, trojans, and other malicious malware attacking our systems. But the big change is that the first early virus writers were nearly all misguided youths (they didn't have any motive other than to create trouble). These so-called "script kiddies" didn't make any money out of their malware. This is no longer the case!

In early 2000, there was a big shift in the way computer malware was spread. Numerous self-replicating computer worms exploited part of the Windows operating system, infecting huge numbers of Microsoft powered servers and desktops worldwide. At the time there were very few firewalls installed and most servers were open to the Internet. Infection was simple as system updates were done manually so computer worms could exploit the many unpatched systems.

By the mid-2000s malware transitioned from being nuisance motivated to profit driven. This changed everything, and malware driven cyber crime started to develop. The first email phishing campaigns started around this time and mass spammers spreading malware became a major problem.

The days of the lone, trouble-making, misguided hacker are long gone. Replacing them are professional, skillful malware coders, profit focused cyber criminals, and armies of determined hackers and exploiters.

As the Internet continues to make the world a smaller place, it has also made it easy for those with time and technical skills to get online and launch attacks from almost anywhere. While China, Russia, Ukraine, Romania, the United States, and Brazil are considered the biggest hotbeds for cyber criminal gang activity, they are not alone.[50] Organized crime combined with mass youth unemployment is helping to contribute to the growing number of malicious hackers that can now be found across many Eastern European, Asian, Middle Eastern, and Latin American countries.

Cyber Crime as a Growth Industry

In 2012 Symantec, the makers of the Norton range of security products, estimated the global direct cash costs of cyber crime (money stolen or spent resolving cyber attacks) to be $114 billion per annum.[51] In 2014 McAfee estimated cyber crime cost the global economy closer to $400 billion.[52] No matter who you ask, all agree cyber crime is continuing to grow. While estimates on the size of the actual cyber criminal market vary, all agree it is a huge, global threat that's growing rapidly.

In their 2015 Global Security Report, Trustwave looked at the Return-on-Investment (ROI) that continues to make cyber crime attractive to computer savvy individuals and criminal gangs. They estimated a cyber criminal spending around $6,000 buying ransomware malware, gaining Internet traffic and resources, stands to make approximately 1,425% ROI in 30 days. That's one reason cyber crime is booming, it can be highly profitable.[53]

Other examples include:

- When the FBI closed down the Estonian Rove Digital cyber criminal team in 2011, it was estimated they had earned $14 million from their spam and trojan distribution activities.

- In 2010 a U.S. cyber crime network was shut down that had stolen over $70 million by using Zeus trojans to steal online banking information. Their range of victims included individuals, small businesses, municipalities, and churches.

All Data Has Value

Data has become a form of currency and there is a ready market for almost any information that can be stolen. Criminals either sell or trade the data they steal or use it to perpetuate other crimes.

Point-of-sale Hacks

During 2014 and throughout 2015 there have been numerous large point-of-sale system breaches. Companies such as Target, Home Depot, Dairy Queen, Jimmy Johns, Neiman Marcus, and numerous others have had their systems breached. This has resulted in massive amounts of stolen credit and debit card data.

This stolen information is sold on Darknet hacker forums. This is a part of the Internet that most people will never see—a world where criminals buy and sell stolen personal information, drugs, malware exploits, and other illegal materials and services.

The data taken from the point-of-sale hacks included all the user information contained in the magnetic strip found on the back of credit and debit cards. This is the card number, the cardholder name, the expiry dates, and the CCV number that's found on the back of the card. Buyers either use the information to make online purchases (where a physical card is not required), or they produce new counterfeit cards for in-store higher-end purchases, buying goods they can sell quickly for cash.

Stolen Personal Information

On the other hand, hackers are interested in a lot more than credit card details. All personal data as well as corporate intellectual property can be sold on different Darknet forums. For instance, stolen personal information can also be used to produce forged driver licenses, passports, and other fake immigration and ID documents.

An estimated 800 Darknet forums and Internet marketplaces list stolen identities for sale. A full identity including name, date-of-birth, SSN, address, other contact details, and credit card information is referred to as a "fullz." Factors that determine the price the criminals sell it for include: the amount of credit the stolen identity can be used to apply for as well as how recent and complete the data is. Prices for "fullz" range from $1 to over $400 each. The average price seems to be around $20.

Tools of the Trade

Cyber thieves have a varied bag of tools at their disposal. These include various forms of malware and using social engineering tricks to steal from their victims.

Malware

"Malware" comes from the words "MALiscious" and "softWARE.. It's a catch-all term used to describe numerous different categories of maliciously designed computer code.

It's impossible to calculate the number of individual computer viruses, worms, and trojans as new ones are constantly being written. Independent security lab AV-Test estimates that nearly 400 million individual malicious programs have been written since 1984, with the vast majority of these occurring in the last three years. They estimate around 390,000 new malicious program samples are registered with them every day! Many samples are similar to already known malware programs; however, on average there are 14,000 new malware programs every month.

There are numerous types of malware which include:

- Trojans that disguise themselves as legitimate files, while containing hidden malicious payloads. Normally these are spread by phishing campaigns where users are fooled into opening attachments that contain trojans downloaded by the user.

- Viruses are based on the concept of a biological virus. They infect devices and reproduce themselves. Viruses are self-spreading, moving from infected device to device.

- Worms produce copies of themselves and replicate over networks to vulnerable connected systems. Some worms target and replicate via instant messaging.

- Rootkits are a type of malware that hides deep in the system. Rootkits are activated when a system boots up, before the operating system has completely started, and are often overlooked by anti-malware detection.

- Spyware tracks your online activity without your knowledge, often monitoring your online browsing, chats, emails, and buying habits. Spyware loaded on a mobile device can also track where you go. Spyware is sometimes included with legitimate software when it's downloaded and it's covered in the privacy policy. The developers are taking a chance that most will never read the software agreements and will click and accept. So spyware is loaded with your consent!

- Key-loggers run in the background stealing information that the user types. They are used by criminals to capture user credit card numbers, names, passwords, and other account login information.

- Adware often comes bundled with free software. It works by re-directing users to specific websites, delivering ads, or hi-jacking your browser homepage and replacing it with one chosen by the adware. Many downloads include toolbars which are deeply embedded and difficult to remove. Some adware monitors your Internet activity sending reports to remote servers.

Nearly all malware disrupts and degrades the performance of your system and most steal or destroy data. Most malware relies on human weakness or unpatched systems to infect the victim's devices. Cyber criminals know how to trick users into opening attachments and following links that will ultimately lead to their machine becoming infected.

Crypting

The malware development market is highly sophisticated with teams constantly developing new strains and improving existing malware. In order to ensure their code won't be detected as malicious by anti-malware software, it's tested before release. Malware writers do this by submitting their newly written software to a so-called "crypting service." Crypting services are a lucrative sector for criminals. They add custom encryption to obfuscate their malware by testing it against all leading anti-malware scanners to ensure none can detect it as being harmful.[54] This can often take several tries before the software will get past the scanners. Once they are satisfied the software is ready, the crypting service sends the malware code back to the writers. They will either use it for attacks or sell it to other cyber criminals on underground web forums.

It's not only cyber criminals who write and spread malware. There are several other groups who are actively involved in writing malware or attacking computer systems.

Government Produced Malware
Government intelligence agencies from many nations are also active developers of malware. Their wares are mainly used for spying purposes in an ongoing and ever-expanding digital "cold war."

2003 was the first time that targeted government sponsored malware was seen. A Word document containing a hidden exploit was deliberately emailed, targeting a defense contractor in Europe in an attempt to steal confidential data. All evidence suggested that the malware was written by and sent from a Chinese government hacker in order to spy and steal military secrets. Similar targeted attacks are still practiced today using tailor-made spying malware coming from China. This modern form of espionage is currently an ongoing problem for almost every first world nation.

The Chinese government is certainly not alone in writing malware although they are one of the main culprits. Other countries engaged in the same activities include, but are not limited to, the USA, Russia, Iran, and North Korea as well as probably Israel, India, Pakistan, Taiwan, Germany, and South Korea and others.

Most government malware is written to exploit vulnerabilities that haven't been made known to the public. These are called zero-day attacks, because no anti-malware will detect them and no patches have been developed. Often once a victim's computer has been infected, a remotely accessible backdoor can be created. Other common tactics include attackers creating fictitious new user accounts and escalating user privileges in order to gain access to different parts of the network. This allows them to search for and steal confidential company documents. Or they may simply read all documents and emails on the system, staying hidden for years. Zero-day attacks are definitely responsible for some major espionage and spying. For example, the NSA recently revealed that the Chinese government has been targeting and accessing the private emails of top Obama Administration officials since before 2010.[55]

Unless you are a journalist, an activist, or a political figure, there is not much chance you will be targeted by government hackers in your personal capacity. However, if you work for the military, are involved in technology or biotech research (of almost any kind), or work in a government department, there is a good chance you could be a target. In fact, even if you are friends with anyone who works for the government, you could be a target and used as a "side door" to get at your contacts.

Another one of the favorite methods used by government spies is to target the social media contacts of foreign governments. With the hope of infecting the social media and email accounts of their friends, they can then send targeted infected spear phishing emails to their intended government employee victim.

Hacktivism
Hacktivists are individuals who write malware as a form of online civil disobedience. Groups are normally loosely organized and work together to attack companies and organizations they disagree with. Hacktivist attacks are related to issues of free speech, anti-capitalism, political protest, and human rights.

Hacktivist tactics include disrupting websites with denial-of-service attacks, defacing websites, and publishing sensitive documents in order to embarrass organizations or individuals (such as on sites like Wikileaks).

The most notorious hacktivist group is Anonymous who have been involved with numerous attacks on government, corporate, and religious websites.

Some hacktivist groups in addition to disrupting online services and websites, also target individuals working for the military, governments, religious organizations, law enforcement, and certain companies the group is "protesting" against.

As hacking skills and exploit kits proliferate online, hacktivism looks set to become a bigger issue.

Different Malware Attacks

Cyber criminals and hackers often combine different types of malware together for innovative attacks and are constantly designing new ones. Here are some examples to give an overview of how different types of malware attacks work:

- Banking trojans
- Ransomware
- Botnets
- Bitnets

Banking Trojans

Malware trojans are based on the same concept used by the ancient Greeks when they employed a benign looking horse statue to enter the ancient city of Troy. Just as the original Trojan horse fooled the inhabitants of Troy, malware trojans look harmless while carrying hidden malicious code.

Banking trojans are a specifically written class of malware designed to steal online banking user name and password combinations. They come disguised looking like a useful image, document, PDF, or other kind of file typically via email attachment. Once opened they either infect the device or direct it to download additional malicious software.

How the Fraud Works
There are typically several different groups of players involved in banking trojan criminal fraud rings. First there are the actual malware coders who develop the software and offer it for sale to hackers. There is an active illicit underground market for banking trojans, accessible only via TOR on the Darknet. The actual hackers who purchase the trojans use them to snare victims. The last group involved is the money mules. These individuals help transfer stolen funds, keeping back a percentage of the ill-gotten gains for themselves.

Phishing emails are a favorite form of malware delivery. User devices can also become infected by trojans. While visiting a legitimate website that has been hijacked, it automatically re-directs them to a site where numerous exploit kits are waiting for them. A so-called drive-by download takes place, delivering the malware unnoticed to the victim's machine. In most cases the malware exploit will take advantage of unpatched vulnerabilities in products like Java, Flash, PDF reader, media players, and other plugins. *(See section on updating applications to ensure all applications and browser plug-ins are kept updated.)*

Banking trojans that have infected computers can also be transferred to smartphones and tablets when they are connected by USB cable during charging.

Banking trojans mostly comprised of a rootkit are disguised to remain unnoticed and undetected for as long as possible. Trojans can be developed to do almost anything on a device as long as the account they operate under has administration rights. They can steal information, download software, make changes to application settings, record keystrokes as they are typed on the keyboard, monitor

Internet usage, and collect personal information. In an effort to remain operational, some banking trojans are designed to not only steal financial information but also identify and remove anti-malware software from the infected machine. Many banking trojans will sit inactive on the device waiting for the user to log into a bank or other financial account. This activates the trojan, which then attempts to either steal the banking credentials or change the account numbers to steal funds directly out of the user's account. Mobile versions of banking trojan malware have been designed that try and steal the one-time security codes delivered by banks to approve transfers.

If the target for the trojan is to steal financial login data, once it has collected the targeted data, it will often encrypt and exfiltrate (export in the background so as to stay hidden) the information to a remote command server typically somewhere in Eastern Europe or Russia.

Once the attackers collect the stolen login credentials they can then access the victim's account and transfer funds directly out of the bank account to their money mules. The money mules then transfer the funds to the hackers, keeping their cut.

One of the most notorious banking trojans was a nasty program named ZeuS. Before the main hacker behind ZeuS was captured in 2013, his software was used to steal over $100 million from more than 120 U.S. banks over a 5-year period.

Organized cyber crime rings are developing newer, more sophisticated banking trojans all the time. Most use a combination of phishing methods to trick users into downloading their malware. With so many huge data breaches of personal information, deceptive personal spear phishing campaigns aimed at high net worth individuals are a big concern.

Banking trojan malware reached an all-time high in 2014. As more of us use our smartphones to conduct online banking, malware writers have followed. Numerous mobile banking trojans, especially those that attack Android devices, are doing the rounds as criminals have developed their wares for mobile devices.

Ransomware

Ransomware is another fast growing and particularly nasty class of malicious malware, proving to be highly profitable for cyber criminals. The objective of ransomware is to hold user's data hostage in an attempt to extort a fine or "ransom." Some ransomware will even drop child pornography onto your hard drive and then demand you pay a fine. While rates vary, approximately 35% of people infected with ransomware trojans pay the ransom in order to retrieve their data.

There are two basic kinds of ransomware—locker and crypto ransomware.

Locker ransomware first appeared around 2011, locking device screens while displaying a fake official message (often designed to look as if it was from the FBI or another police department) demanding a fine be paid. (Note the FBI and law enforcement don't lock user computer screens and demand fines.) Authoritative wording is often used to make the threat look like an authentic law enforcement notice in an attempt to get victims to pay up.

In 2013 ransomware moved from locking device screens to encrypting files. This scam encrypts all the user's data and image files. Plus in some versions, it also locks any attached storage devices or shared drives. Crypto ransomware is designed to extort a ransom fine in exchange for the decryption key, which is held by the attackers. If the initial ransom amount isn't paid in the time period that the criminals demand, anywhere from 72 hours to a week, the amount requested increases. If after an extended period no payment is made, the private key required to undo the encryption is deleted and the data lost.

Most ransomware payments are made using Bitcoin. Some of the scammers even run helpdesks to assist their victims in buying Bitcoin so they can make the ransom payment. They may even go another step and provide a helpdesk to assist the victims in decrypting their hard drives and getting their files back. The reason being if they don't, then no one will pay them. However, they rightly understand if they help users retrieve their documents, this will encourage more victims to pay up and they will earn more money from their scam. Reputation it seems is even important to cyber criminals.

While ransomware has been around for many years, its effectiveness has spurred newer and more sophisticated versions from malware developers. Historically, most ransomware has targeted users of Microsoft Windows desktops. Newer versions are now being written to target mobile phones. One interesting example is Android/Locker.CBltr, which not only locks your phone screen while claiming to be from the FBI, it also takes over your camera and snaps a photo of you while demanding you pay a "fine" of $500.

A quick look at some of the other most notorious ransomware trojans:

CryptoLocker: The CryptoLocker trojan was the first major example of ransomware when it appeared in September 2013. It targeted all versions of Windows from XP through to Windows 8. It was estimated that in the first 100 days after release it infected around 250,000 systems worldwide. In May 2014, the Gameover Zeus botnet, which had been used to distribute the CryptoLocker trojan, was taken down in a joint FBI/Interpol operation that was joined by several security vendors and universities. As a result of hacking software recovered from some of the servers used to control the botnet, two of the security vendors, Fox-IT and FireEye, were able to offer a recovery service to anyone who had files encrypted with CryptoLocker. *(See Take Action Steps: Ransomware section below.)* After the takedown it was estimated that 41% of victims had paid the "ransom" to get their files back. While the total amount of money paid out to hackers behind CryptoLocker attacks will never be known, in an attempt to calculate a cost, ZD NET traced four Bitcoin addresses used to make ransom payments.[56] In a two month period in late 2013, around $27 million was paid, making CryptoLocker a highly profitable malware exploit.

Due to the success of the original CryptoLocker malware, several ransomware trojans were released which named themselves CryptoLocker. None of them are related to the original, which is no longer operational.

CryptoWall: CryptoWall is a major file encrypting ransomware trojan that affects Windows based systems from XP onward. It's typically spread via spam emails with infected attachments or hosted on compromised websites waiting to infect browsers with outdated plug-ins. In all cases the users are unaware they have been infected until they find themselves locked out of their data by which time it's too late. Once CryptoWall encrypts data, it makes a copy of the files, encrypts the copy, and securely deletes the original files so they can't be recovered with file recovery tools.

Typical CryptoWall infections require $500 to be paid in order to retrieve the decryption key and recover the files. If the ransom is not paid within 72 hours, the ransom amount is increased to $1,000. If no payment is made after a week, the decryption keys required to recover the files are deleted and the data is lost. Between April 2014 when it was first seen and June 2015, the FBI's Internet Crime Complaint Center (IC3) recorded victims losing over $18 million due to CryptoWall.

Ransomware is here to stay. Ransomware has proven to be a lucrative form of cyber crime. Therefore, we will probably have to deal with it for the foreseeable future.

Despite some law enforcement success in disrupting the supply and infrastructure used by ransomware criminals, in January 2015 the FBI released an alert warning due to the increasing rise in ransomware attacks, especially those focused on mobile devices.[57]

Ransomware trojans have also already made the jump to Internet connected TVs. In the future, many IoT connected devices, smart homes and even smart cars, are likely to be targets for ransomware attacks. So if you hear of someone late to a meeting because their car was hacked and held for ransom, don't be surprised.

Ransomware: Take Action Steps

Prevention is much better than the cure when dealing with ransomware. The best form of protection is of course not to get infected in the first place.

- Ensure you are making regular backups of all important data files. As connected drives can also be attacked, disconnected backups are a key part of any defense.

- Keep anti-malware/endpoint protection updated at all times (including for all mobile devices).

- Ensure your system and applications are always patched with the latest updates. Drive-by downloads that exploit vulnerabilities in outdated web browser plug-ins are one way to get infected.

- Don't open attachments you are not expecting.

- Don't click on links in unsolicited emails.

- If your system gets infected with ransomware, don't pay the ransom. In most cases, the criminals will release your files, but not always. Paying only encourages the bad guys to continue developing and attacking more people. Deleting the infected files and restoring from backups is the best option.

- If you don't have current backups, there are some file recovery tools that may work. Examples are:
  - o R-Studio (http://www.r-studio.com)
  - o Recuva (http://www.piriform.com/recuva)
  - o PhotoRec (http://www.cgsecurity.org/wiki/PhotoRec)

- If you don't have current backups and aren't able to recover, paying the criminals may be your only choice to recover your data.
  - o If you do decide to pay up, do so sooner rather than later. Most amounts required double after a period of time, sometimes as short s only 72 hours.

- Report all ransomware attacks to the FBI's Internet Crime Complaint Center (http://www.ic3.gov).

- If files were encrypted by CryptoLocker, FireEye and Fox IT (two security vendors) developed a solution to unencrypt files at this link: https://www.decryptcryptolocker.com

- For technically advanced users, Foolish IT has developed a utility called CryptoPrevent. This will set Windows policies to protect devices from some ransomware malware. There is a basic fee to use utility and more advanced paid for editions. CryptoPrevent works on all versions of Windows from XP to Version 10: https://www.foolishit.com/cryptoprevent-malware-prevention/

Large numbers of malware-infected machines can be harnessed into a so-called "botnet." This is a network of online infected drones that can be centrally controlled. Botnets can be used for various nefarious activities while the owners of the computers remain unaware of the activity. The only indication they may have in noticing that something is different is the slow speed of their systems as their computing resources are being stolen. Botnets are used to spread malware often by sending out huge amounts of spam. An example is the notorious Cutwail botnet, which for years has been used to deliver numerous types of malware via infected spam. At one point it was estimated to have over 2 million infected drone "bots" sending out up to 74 billion spam emails every day. Some control servers have been taken down; however, the Cutwail botnet is still operating and being offered for rent by hackers on the Russian Darknet.

Botnets are also instrumental in being part of distributed denial-of-service attacks (DDoS). DDoS attacks bombard websites with repeated requests in order to overwhelm and knock them offline. This prevents legitimate users from accessing them.

Cyber criminals rent out botnets of infected devices to attack any target they get paid to attack. According to *Wired* magazine you can hire a DDoS botnet for as little as $2 an hour or buy one for around $700 courtesy of the Russian hacking underground.[58]

Bitnet

A "Bitnet" (not to be confused with the Bitcoin payments company of the same name) is a botnet of malware infected machines used to mine easy to create cyber currencies such as Lite coin or Doggie coin. The criminals then convert the cyber currency to Bitcoin before further converting to Russian rubles or U.S. currency. The cyber thieves in Bitnet attacks are targeting the computing power of the devices they infect with mining malware.

In early 2014, Yahoo's homepage was tricked into serving Bitcoin malware hidden in ads[59] to over 2 million European website visitors. Innovative cyber criminals have also used other methods to spread their wares, such as loading numerous apps on Google Play that contain hidden Bitcoin-mining malware[60] as well as using Skype to spam mining malware to victims.[61]

Social Engineering

Social engineering is the term used to describe the way criminals use deception to gain the keys to the kingdom. Social engineering can be done in person, over the phone, via the Internet, through emails, or messaging.

Social engineers use a combination of impersonation, manipulation, deception, and misdirection to gain access where they shouldn't be allowed, to gather and steal information from their victims.

Criminals use social engineering tactics because they work. It's usually easier to exploit your natural inclination to trust than it is to discover ways to hack into your accounts. For example, it is much easier to trick someone into giving you their password than it is to try hacking their password (unless of course their password is really weak).

It's largely believed that several of the most recent high-profile security breaches started with cyber criminals using social engineering to gain access to their targets. These include the well-publicized attacks at Target, Home Depot, Experian, eBay, and JPMorgan. It's also likely that the Sony hack probably began by the attackers using some form of social engineering to get into the network.

Common tools include:

- Phishing (see section below).

- Vishing or voice phishing are phone calls to gather information or trick users by impersonating a trusted resource or someone with authority. For instance, a caller pretending they are from a bank or technology company helpdesk and asking for the user's login details. Another tactic is to pretend your system is infected with a virus and they claim they can remove it. If you saw the movie *Identity Thief*, that's exactly what Melissa McCarthy's character did to Jason Bateman when she stole his ID. If this ever happens to you, don't engage, simply tell them to get lost and hang up, it's a scam!

Phishing Attacks

Phishing is a form of an email based social engineering attack. It works by criminals sending emails that appear to be harmless but are not. As a category, phishing is responsible for approximately 22% of all cyber criminal attacks.

Email spoofing is a commonly used tactic in phishing email attacks. This entails changing the "from email address" to make the email look like it comes from a friend, co-worker, or other trusted source. They hope to overcome any hesitation to opening attachments or following links. This is how spammers worked for many years before good spam filters became available.

Phishing emails use actual logos and wording lifted directly from a company website to make the phishing attacks look realistic. In June 2015, the top brands used on fake phishing websites to fool users were Facebook, Google, mail.com, Mail.ru, Telstra, CNBC, Groupon, LinkedIn, Conrad.nl, and Road Runner.[62]

There are numerous variations to phishing attacks, and cyber criminals are constantly improving and refining their techniques to better fool and manipulate victims. Phishing attacks are often timed to coincide with major sports events or world news. For instance during the FIFA World Cup, the Olympic Games, the Super Bowl, and other major events, criminals try to fool sports fans into opening emails and clicking on links to fake websites. Likewise, natural disasters like hurricanes and earthquakes trigger phishing campaigns with cyber criminals attempting to use current events to overcome user caution.

Phishing attacks are also seasonal with a huge increase towards the end of the year with lots of holiday themed phishing emails going around.

Successful cyber criminals are smart and good at what they do. They put a lot of time and effort into creating compelling email messages designed to deceive users. And their efforts often work very well. The numbers bear this out. Phishers play a numbers game. They know on average the percentage of people who will click on links and the percentage of those who will be fooled into entering their credentials on fake websites.

Among the most common phishing tactics are:

- An email containing a link to an infected website. Typically if the link is clicked, the user is directed to a fake website where they will be tricked into downloading malicious code, or a web exploit loaded on the site will automatically infect the device if it's not patched and updated.

- A variation on the attack is to present the user with a fake login screen to a website they trust. The scammers hope the victim won't notice that the website is a fake and will enter their login and password. The phisher then uses stolen details on the real website to gain access to the victim's account.

- Another kind of attack is to include a malware infected attachment in the email. The user opens the attachment and it infects their system with malicious software. Malware writers are very good at making attachments look legitimate by changing the description of the attachment and editing the file icons. Plus they know many users too often simply click yes to make any warning prompts go away.

Phishing: Take Action Steps

To protect yourself from phishing attacks, watch out for the following:

- When it comes to email, being a bit paranoid is fine. If an email looks odd or the language is a bit strange, text or call the person who sent it to you before opening any attachments or clicking any links.

- If you ever get an email asking you to reset your password or confirm your details ignore it, that's a phishing attempt.

- Beware of emails asking for "urgent help" from friends stuck somewhere. Creating a sense of urgency is an attempt to get the user to make a mistake without thinking. A similar tactic is telling you one of your accounts is about to be blocked unless you follow the link to reset it, etc. Don't take the bait.

- Any emails claiming you have won a prize, the lottery, or have an inheritance to claim and asking you to confirm your details are a scam.

- Never buy anything from spam emails. Chances are it's either a fake item or a phishing attempt.

- Never click on links or open attachments from strangers or from anyone you are not expecting to get attachments from.

- Never click on links in emails from your bank or a company you do business with. Rather open a new browser tab, type in their url, and go directly to their website.

- Be aware of receiving attached "invoices" for items you have not ordered or received. Although this kind of attack is mostly aimed at companies, it could be used on individuals as well.

- Smart phishers may sometimes combine attacks by using a spoofed email, followed up with a vishing (fake) phone call in an attempt to get users to take action. If in doubt, take the caller's name, department, and number and hang up. DON'T call back the number they gave you, rather call the company's main number and check if the call was legitimate.

Phone Phishing Attacks

Cyber criminals are ever inventing new ways to scam users and steal from them. Phone phishing attacks are designed to take over email accounts where only an email and mobile phone number are known. (Both are easy for cyber criminals to obtain. [63]) The attack works like this:

- An attacker wishes to gain access to an email account that uses SMS text message verification to reset passwords (like Gmail, Yahoo, and Outlook).

- The attacker goes to the email account, enters the email address, and clicks on the "need help" link that is used by email account holders who have forgotten their passwords.

- The attacker chooses "get a verification code on my phone" and enters the mobile phone number of the account holder.

- The account holder gets a code text from the email provider, Gmail in this case.

- The attacker then sends the phishing SMS text message "this is Google, there has been some unauthorized activity on your account. Please reply with your verification code."

- If the email account holder sends the code back thinking they are verifying their account, they have just given the attacker the code needed to access their email account and lock them out.

Phone Phishing: Take Action Steps

To protect yourself from phone phishing attacks, watch out for the following:

- Be aware of unsolicited SMS text messages containing or asking you for verification codes.

- If you think it is legitimate, always check with your email provider.

- Recovery password phone text services never require a response.

Identify theft has been the leading issue topping the FTC's consumer complaint rankings for 15 years straight.

It's easy to see why. From late 2013, large data breaches exposed the personal information (including: Social Security numbers, emails, names, dates of birth, full addresses, health history, financial history, and in some cases fingerprints) of nearly half of all U.S. adults.

Large breaches occurred at the following organizations:

U.S. Government—Anyone who has applied for a job or worked for the Federal government since 2000 was affected.
- Office of Personnel Management data breach.

Websites
- Adobe
- AOL
- eBay
- LivingSocial
- Slack
- Snapchat
- Twitch
- Twitter

Health Insurance providers
- Anthem
- Care First
- CHS
- Premera

Retailers—Point-of-sale hacks affecting anyone who used a credit or debit card at the following businesses (*Note: not all branches of each company were affected):*

- Albertsons (June 2014 - July 2014)

- Dairy Queen (August 2014 – September 2014)
- Goodwill Stores (February 2013 – August 2014)
- The Home Depot (April 2014 – September 2014)
- Kmart (September 2014 – October 2014)
- Michaels (May 2013 – January 2014)
- Neiman Marcus (July 2013 – October 2013)
- P.F. Chang (February 2014 – June 2014)
- Sally Beauty (March 2014 – April 2015)
- Staples (July 2014 – September 2014)
- Supervalu (June 2014 – July 2014)
- Target (November 2013 – December 2013)
- UPS Stores (January 2014 – August 2014)

These are only the big cases that made news headlines. Year-to-date in 2015 (January to July), the Identity Theft Resource Center (ITRC) reported 450 data breaches, with 135,257,677 personal data records exposed.[64]

Credit Monitoring Services

Many companies that suffer a data breach will now offer free monitoring services to those customers who may have been affected. In the case of the recent government OPM data breach, 22 million people have been offered credit monitoring for a period of 3 years.

Credit monitoring/protection services monitor your credit record and inform you of any changes. For example, they will alert you if someone tries to open new credit cards or accounts in your name. Some credit monitoring services also let you know if there is an attempt to change the address on your bank account. While services differ widely, some offer legal fee reimbursements and insurance in the event of fraud. (Although the same is offered for free under existing credit card with their zero liability rules.)

Be aware an issue many people have with credit-monitoring services is in order for them to be able to monitor all your accounts, you need to provide a lot of additional information to them, including but not limited to passport, medical, and bank account information and numbers. For many privacy minded individuals who are already victims of identity theft, having to hand out a lot more personal information to yet another big company doesn't always sit well with them.

Unfortunately, credit-monitoring services offer little in the way of actually stopping ID theft. The key issue is that they also don't stop new credit accounts from being opened in your name. Should this happen, it will eventually lead to your credit being ruined. In most cases when you get the report, it will be too late to stop the new account from being opened. You will see the trail of an event after it has happened. However, you will be able to start quickly repairing any damage as most credit-monitoring services help with cleaning up after your stolen data has been used to ruin your credit report.

A few things most credit-monitoring services don't do include:

- Monitoring your bank account, brokerage, retirement, and other financial accounts.

- They are not able to stop other kinds of fraud including tax refund fraud, Social Security fraud, welfare and other Medicare fraud.

- Monitor your stolen identity, checking any fraudulent applications to apply for new forms of identity such as passports, driver's licenses, and other identity documents.

Credit Freeze
For many privacy minded individuals, a far better solution is to contact the consumer credit reporting agencies and request a freeze be placed on your credit file. A security freeze will prevent anyone who may have stolen your identity from

being able to open a new line of credit or account in your name. This will stop any new creditor from pulling (viewing) your credit file. New and unauthorized accounts can't be opened in your name.

Most security freezes remain in operation until you personally remove or unlock them. If you need to open a new account while the security freeze is in place, a PIN can be used to temporary unlock the service. While some states differ, in general if you have been the victim of identity theft or are older than 65, there is no charge to add or remove a security freeze on your credit file. In most cases however, each credit rating agency charges a nominal fee of around $10 to place or remove a freeze. When compared to the cost and time of having to clean up after identity theft, a security freeze placed at all of the credit agencies is well worth the small cost involved.

The four main consumer credit reporting agencies to contact are:
- Trans Union
- Equifax
- Experian
- Innovis

While placing a freeze at the four major credit rating agencies won't stop 100% of identity theft, it should stop most.

An additional benefit of freezing your credit files is it helps to keep your file clean from inaccurate data. When thieves try and open new accounts in your name, it can pollute your credit file with incorrect data. For instance, if a fraudster tries to open a new line of credit in your name and only has partial information, they may add the wrong address or phone number, which often gets added into your credit file. It can be a time-consuming process to erase the incorrect information and involves contacting each individual credit-reporting agency.

Tax return fraud is another growing problem. Fraudsters have targeted IRS tax refunds by filing fraudulent returns and pocketing the refunds. The U.S. Government Accountability Office has confirmed over $6 billion is paid out in fraudulent returns annually. Tax return fraud is now seen as a standard crime. Gangster rap songs tell how easy it is to steal people's identity and submit false returns. Law enforcement has been rather slow at combatting this easy to commit crime. But with the huge sums of money stolen, this needs their attention.

In the past, one of the ways criminals were able to steal refunds from the IRS was by targeting the IRS's online past tax transcript website. This website was set up to allow taxpayers to get copies of their most recently filed tax records. Armed with stolen personal information, including names, date of birth, Social Security numbers, and filing status, of 610,000 victims of identity theft, the criminals were able to successfully retrieve over 330,000 transcripts. Once they had the previous transcripts in hand, they used the information to fraudulently file tax returns for 2015 and steal the IRS refunds. As the IRS became aware that some accounts were receiving numerous refunds, the criminals simply switched tactics and got refunds channeled to money mules (or drop hoes as they call them), who passed the refunds, minus a cut, onto the low-life criminals.

Unfortunately, it's not only outsiders pulling this scam. In June 2015, the IRS announced one of their own employees had stolen the identities of 350 people that she had access to. She used this information to file fraudulent returns and netted $326,000 in tax refunds. So the moral of the story is to file your taxes early before someone else uses your information. If you e-file and your submission is rejected due to taxes already filed under your SSN, you know fraudsters have beaten you to it!

If your e-file tax filing online is rejected due to your SSN already being used, you need to file a paper return plus follow the steps below.

If you believe you are the victim of identity theft or IRS tax refund fraud, follow the steps below to report the tax fraud to the IRS and the police:

- File a police report if you're a victim of tax refund fraud.

- File a complaint with the Federal Trade Commission on their website if you're a victim of tax refund fraud.

- Call the IRS Identity Protection Specialized Unit at 1-800-908-4490 for guidance.

- Complete Form 14039-Identity Theft Affidavit to prove that you are the real taxpayer (or on behalf of a deceased spouse or relative whose personal information was used to obtain a fraudulent tax refund).
    o If you're a victim of identity theft and the theft is affecting your tax records, check Box 1 in Section A. However, if your identity was compromised but it was not used on a fraudulent tax filing, check Box 2 in Section A. (You can also check this box if you had any personal belongings or Social Security cards stolen.)

- Mail Form 14039 to this address: Internal Revenue Service, Stop C2003, Fresno, CA 93888

In order to help combat this problem, the IRS has implemented an enhanced authentication scheme. Certain taxpayers can receive a six-digit Identity Protection Personal

Identification Number (IP PIN) to help prevent fraudulent tax filings in their name. The IP PIN must be included on all future returns. If your private data has been stolen, without the PIN number you are protected from anyone filing under your name.

This scheme is currently only available to individuals who have either been a victim of identity theft or those who are residents of Florida, Georgia, or Washington, D.C. (all states with high rates of Federal tax refund fraud). (Note these PINs only apply to Federal and not to state tax filings.) Hopefully this program will be rolled out to other areas.

- If you qualify for your IRS IP PIN, look on the IRS website for more information: http://www.irs.gov/Individuals/Get-An-Identity-Protection-PIN

Social Security Benefit Fraud

Just like the above-mentioned IRS tax refund fraud, the Social Security benefit system is also open to abuse by fraudsters. The Social Security Administration (SSA) online management portal is often targeted by fraudsters intent on hijacking Social Security payments of those who haven't yet registered at the SSA website. By using stolen personally identifiable information, they can create online SSA accounts and divert payments to their bank accounts.

Another method used to gain access by criminals is by use of phishing emails to fool citizens into creating accounts at fake Social Security websites.

All emails from government departments end with .gov/ (with a forward slash / always following the .gov). Phishing attempts will try and fool users into entering their details on false websites using .gov but with additional letters like this: .gov.gmx.com/ or .gov.bx.co.rx/setup. Any sites that look like this are fake. If in doubt, don't follow the links but rather go straight to the official Social Security site at http://www.socialsecurity.gov/

SSN Benefit Fraud: Take Action Steps

A good way to ensure that no false account is opened in your name is to open one yourself. Since only one account can be tied to a SSN, this blocks any fraudster from using the system to access your account.

- Go to my Social Security (http://www.ssa.gov/myaccount/) and create your online account before anyone else does using your stolen SSN.

Chapter 7

Tracked, Attacked, and Fighting Back

"Users should become more aware of how visible their personal data is online, more aware of who has access to it, and more aware of how it can be used against them."
IBM® X-Force Trend & Risk Report

Today there is no such thing as privacy without planning and good security. If you want to keep or regain your privacy, you have to take responsibility for it.

Securing your privacy and data isn't a once-off process either, but rather a layered multi-step approach. For example, picture a castle—there is a moat, several walls, and multiple defensive positions to deter attackers. In a similar fashion, you will need to correct your behavior (no more giving your data away), secure your systems, update your software, and use security and privacy products to defeat those who are tracking and attempting to hack you. Lastly, you need to stay alert to new threats and scams.

Securing Your Thinking

The very first step in securing yourself is to secure your thinking. You have to decide how much privacy and data protection you want to have. To help you do this, you need to think about how your personally identifiable data is currently being collected and used. Then understand that what you share today could be used in the future.

109

Privacy is personal. Some people don't seem to be bothered about who knows private details about them. Others go to great lengths to ensure their conversations and lifestyles are kept private.

However, no matter how careful or concerned you are or are not about your privacy, unless you know who and how you are being tracked, you can't make a qualified decision.

Take the Long-term View

We are told that elephants don't forget. Well I'm not certain about that, but I'm very sure that the Internet doesn't forget anything even if you forgot that you posted it. Once comments and images are loaded online, they can be found weeks, months, and even years later. Sure with today's search tools it might be hard to filter and find information that was posted a few years ago, but make no mistake in the future it will get easier. As big data query technologies improve, a skilled researcher will be able to search for and find not only what you did last summer, but also the one before that and the one before that! In other words, if the data is out there, it can be found. In most cases you can't take back what you have said or done online. So stop and think BEFORE you post ANYTHING online. Can this info, comment, photo, video, etc. come back and bite you somewhere in the future?

With that in mind, today's teenagers and young adults would be well advised to really think twice or even more times, before posting and making comments online. We may only be in the early stages of social profiling. Unless there are some big changes in terms of legislation, data collection, and analysis, profiling will continue to grow and get easier. The big data society is here to stay. The best protection is to not post online in the first place.

110

Plan and Take Action

Your personal privacy and data security plan starts here. Depending on the level of your desire for privacy, there are different solutions. Applying preventative technologies and strategies can go a long way in terms of keeping your data out of the hands of people you would rather didn't have it.

Audit Yourself—Know Where Your Data Is

In order to secure your data, it's vital to conduct a self-assessment on where it is located. To do this you can use all the search tools to see what anyone searching for you would find. Next, you can look at the information the data brokers have collected about you. Lastly, you will put a strategy into place to stop giving your personal data away.

Cleaning Up Your Online Presence

Numerous online websites, search engines, data brokers, online directories, and social media sites all contain our personally identifiable information. This data can be broken into two broad categories: 1) information from public records, and 2) non-public information.

Public record information is not considered confidential. It includes court records, legal settlements and litigation, real estate appraisals, births, marriages and deaths, voter registration (in some states), and more.

Public records can often be obtained by using a Freedom of Information request. That's the bad news if you want to keep your information out of the public view. One of the only ways to protect this information is to put as many assets as possible into trusts or companies. Some states also allow you to keep your information confidential. It's best to always choose that option if possible.

Non-public information is data gathered from commercial entities you do business with and they sell your data.

The number of companies collecting, aggregating, publishing, and selling personal and public records continues to grow. You can segregate this list into several broad categories such as:

- Data brokers, background checkers, online directories, and people finders *(see section on data brokers and actions to take in Chapter 5)*

- Social media and photo sharing sites *(see Chapter 11 for action to take on social media and photo sharing sites)*

Your Face Online

Not only do you need to be aware of your personal information posted in online directories and people finder sites, but you also need to check where images of your face are posted.

With image search engines it's possible to find real names and social media accounts for almost anyone. It's even possible to search and identify people with the image of their face. On dating sites and other forums where people have used an alias, they can still be identified by searching with their facial image.

For instance, Harvard University researcher Adam Tanner wrote in *Forbes* magazine how he copied an image of a young Asian lady from an Indian marriage website and discovered her contact details, professional status, and other details on the social media site LinkedIn. The same method could be applied to images posted on any dating website, probably causing some embarrassment for those who thought they were anonymous hiding behind their online alias.

See facial recognition in Chapter 13.

Online Misinformation Strategy

Although it is considered against the rules of many online services, using a pseudonymous fictitious name can provide some level of anonymity and protection against overt data collection and tracking. Many individuals who are involved in cyber security practice this when online and hide their true identity wherever possible. Writers, who are concerned about protecting their privacy, write blogs and security articles all the time using fake names to protect their real ID.

Is it legal to give out incorrect information?

In most cases there is no legal requirement to provide your true identity and information to social media, online forums and websites unless you are dealing with a financial company, law enforcement, or any part of the Federal or State government.

Online Misinformation: Action Steps

The whole point of using false information is to protect your real identity and provide extra security for your data. Of course, if you create a false persona and forget the details, it will make access to any of your accounts difficult. So make sure you record your false information and keep it locked away in a safe and secure place.

- Create a fake name (alias) to use online

- Create a fake date of birth. Plus stop broadcasting your date of birth on Facebook and other social media accounts. Your real friends and family should know your birthday

- Create a fake place of birth

- Create false answers to be used for secondary security questions. For example: mother's maiden name; name of your favorite sports team; your pet's name; street you grew up on; etc. By using false information here, you will negate anyone who has searched your social media accounts or had access to information that data broking companies have collected on you to find the correct answers to your security questions. Also people who know you may also know the correct answers to these questions and will be able to access your online accounts.

- Specifically create an anonymous email address that you can use when you sign up for online content or services that you would like to use. Most often, when you provide your email address, lots of spam is heading your way. This will allow you to use the service or content without getting all the spam sent directly to your own email address. *(Also see section on "throw-away email" in the email section.)*

- If you need a phone number to sign up for a service, use a temporary throwaway or burner number.
  - See Burner from Ad-Hoc labs (burnerapp.com). It's a temporary, throwaway number app available for use on both Android and iPhones.

Offline Misinformation Strategy

One of the first steps to stop data brokers and advertisers from getting your data is to stop giving your information away. Don't sign up for any new store cards with your real data. Be very hesitant to give your personal data to retailers or anyone

114

else. Even if they do ask for it, don't give your information out unless it's really required.

If you have existing loyalty store cards or accounts, consider closing them. Most companies will provide a way to opt out of receiving their mailers and promotional mailers. If not call their head office and speak to customer service. Ask to be removed from their mailing list and for them to delete your account. Most companies will be willing to comply with your request. (They are legally required to do so by the FCC.) This action will ensure your details are no longer passed along to new data brokers who purchase customer details from them.

Offline Misinformation: Take Action Steps

- When asked by retailers, don't give out your phone number, email, or zip code, etc. Make it a standard practice when checking out anywhere to simply say, "no thanks" when asked for your personal details.

- Pay cash if you don't want any details of your transactions to be collected. Movies tickets, fast food, store purchases, clothing, etc., pay cash for all of them and stop the data brokers (and your credit card company) from adding details of your purchases to your personal profile.

Chapter 8

Secure Your Computer

"If you spend more on coffee than on IT security, you will be hacked. What's more, you deserve to be hacked."
Richard Clarke, former White House Cyber Security Advisor

Secure Your Systems

The first step to keeping your data private and secure from those tracking you is to secure your systems—your computers, tablets, and smartphones that you use to access the Internet. As already mentioned elsewhere in this book, security is all about having multiple layers of defense topped off with common sense. There are numerous privacy enhancing technologies that you can use to secure yourself. The more areas that are covered by security, the greater your overall data protection and privacy will be.

Passwords and Access Control

"The whole notion of passwords is based on an oxymoron. The idea is to have a random string that is easy to remember. Unfortunately, if it's easy to remember, it's something non-random like 'Susan.' And if it's random, like 'r7U2*Qnp,' then it's not easy to remember."
Bruce Schneider, Cyber Security Guru & Author

This quote from Bruce Schneider says it all. Passwords are an integral part of access control, yet it's been shown time and again that most users use ridiculously easy-to-guess

117

passwords. In both the Adobe breach and at more recent website hacks, where massive lists of user passwords have been stolen and decrypted, "123456" and "password" are still the most common passwords for many people!

Passwords

Access control starts with strong passwords. Weak passwords leading to unauthorized access are a major source of data loss for businesses as well as individuals. It cannot be overemphasized how important it is to create strong, unique passwords for each online service you use. Unless you use multi-factor authentication, your password is basically all that stands between your data and a cyber criminal. Interestingly, even hackers themselves often use ridiculously easy to crack passwords. According to a report from AVAST virus labs, they found that hacker passwords weren't any stronger than those used by average computer users.

Over the years we have seen passwords become more numerous, longer, and more complex. So much so that most people forget them or use the same password for multiple accounts. Everyone knows this is not a good idea, yet this is precisely what many users do. In a landmark study conducted several years ago, it was discovered that the average Internet user had 25 separate accounts yet shared only 6 passwords between them. As numerous hacks have shown us, this is not a safe practice.

While brute force password cracking tools are freely available on the Internet, generally malicious hackers are not going to spend hours trying to crack individual passwords. (Unless you are specially targeted.) The most common way for criminals get into accounts is via a data breach for an online service. As happened with Adobe, LinkedIn, Yahoo, eBay, and numerous dubious, so-called "dating sites."

Everyone found out too late that most of the websites that have been hacked were storing user names and passwords in plain text. So the criminals ended up with huge lists of email and password combinations that they could easily test on other sites.

Even when websites "hash" users' passwords (that is apply a cryptographic algorithm that converts the stored plain text password to a string of machine readable characters), it's not always enough. Cyber criminals have found ways around that too. They have large files of stolen cracked passwords and compare the hashed values to obtain the hidden password. This was seen with the 6.5 million LinkedIn stolen passwords. Although they were hashed (not stored in plain readable text), just 6 days after the passwords were stolen, 90% of them had been cracked.[65]

In August 2014, headlines all over the world reported that Russian hackers had amassed over a billion Internet passwords.[66] In fact, the stolen credentials were from 420,000 websites. This further confirms that this is the new way passwords are stolen. We should note that password managers and multi-factor authentication are the only sensible options to secure logins.

Passwords: What Not to Do

With freely available password cracking software, it's easier than ever, given enough time, to brute force crack passwords. So before we look at how to create secure passwords, it's vital to understand what not to include.

Drawn from large hacked access control lists, here is a list of the top "passwords" used by many users. Avoid these at all cost.

- 123456
- password
- 12345
- qwery
- 12345678
- baseball
- abc123

- 111111
- football
- a**hole
- superman
- hockey
- hunter
- harley
- 123456789

In addition to the above, do not use any of the following when choosing a password:

- Don't use real words from a dictionary, either spelled forward or backwards
- Do not use names of songs or movies
- Do not use real names of people or user IDs
- Do not use lists of numbers or letter sequences
- Don't think you can simply replace letters with numbers either, such as a88le instead of apple. Password cracking tools will easily figure this out by using rules to try every combination of every possible number and character to replace the letters.

So bottom line. All real words, regardless of how you spell them are out. In fact there should not be any discernible pattern to your password at all. Password-cracking software will be able to break it wide open.

In addition to the above:

- As many have discovered, using the same email and password combination on multiple accounts is a really bad idea. A web service breach can expose huge numbers of passwords. Cyber criminals then try the same user name and password combinations against commonly used social media, email, ecommerce, and banking websites. It's a known fact that most users still use the same password for numerous accounts. In a recent survey of adults in the UK, more than half admitted to using the same password for all their web forums and online accounts.

- Re-using old passwords is just as bad as having a weak password. Yet this is what too many users do.

How to Create Secure Passwords
Okay, so this is how you create secure passwords:

- **Password length is important.** The length of a password makes a big difference when it comes to cracking it using brute force. It's impossible to determine how long it will take to crack a password. It depends on how much computing power you throw at the problem. However, longer passphrases are better, providing you can remember them!

- Do include a **random combination** of numbers, symbols, upper and lower case characters.

- **Passphrases are better than passwords.** The most secure method, if you are restricted from using numbers and symbols, is to link several random words together into a passphrase that is really long. Like this—oranges, apples, pears and bananas plus "are good for you" would be used as: "*orangesapplespearsandbananasaregoodforyou.*" This is easy to remember and long enough to be secure.

- To further improve the security of this passphrase, you can start with ! and then CAPITILIZE several letters like this with every "A" capitalized: "*!orAngesApplespeArsAndbAnAnAsAregoodforyou*" Sure it's a hassle to write and you might get it wrong, but if you want security, you need secure passwords.

Arguably one of the most important security products you can use is a password manager.

As already mentioned, the big problem we all face with passwords is the difficulty in having to remember them all. The result of having too many passwords is that many users simply use the same or a handful of simple passwords for all or most of their accounts. That's a major bad idea.

Password managers help generate and secure random passwords for each site you access. They allow you to have strong and unique passwords and eliminate the problem of having to remember them. A password manager allows you to specify the length of the password and whether to include symbols and numbers.

Password managers save all account passwords in a secure vault. One master password is all that is required to access the vault. So instead of having to remember dozens of passwords, you only have to remember one, the one to the vault. Adding multi-factor authentication makes access to the secure vault almost impossible for anyone other than you.

Logging into accounts is simple, as the password manger automatically fills in the password from whatever device you are using. In the event that a website is hacked and your password stolen, you simply go and reset your password using the password manager with a new unique secure password.

Additional important features would include the ability to restrict login from any other country except the one in which you live. If you travel, you can update the country settings before leaving.

Are password managers totally secure as they are obviously big juicy targets for thousands of smart hackers? As already mentioned before, there is no such thing as a totally 100% secure system. However, compared to the alternative of having to create your own crazy-long-random-unique numbers and having to recall them all, password managers are a much better option. In fact, in recent research presented at the Symposium on Usable Privacy & Security, a survey showed that 73% of security experts used password managers. This contrasted with only 24% of "non-experts".[67] The results are clear, security professionals recommend and use password managers. I recommend you use one too.

Multi-factored Authentication

Online account access can be made more secure by adding multi-factor authentication. This is an additional form of login verification to the standard user name and password required to gain access to an account or service. Multi-factor authentication is also often referred to as two-factor or dual-factor authentication. My advice is to enable multi-factor authentication wherever you can. It adds security to your standard user name/password combinations.

Multi-factor or two-factor authentication can be provided by numerous means:

- **Hardware tokens**, which are either connected or disconnected. Disconnected tokens have a small screen, which generate and display a different secure number every time the token is used. Many banks and financial firms issue disconnected tokens to their clients. A connected token would be a USB token or a smart card, used in conjunction with a card reader. Connected tokens automatically transmit authentication details when connected to the device.

- **Passcodes**, sometimes also referred to as security codes or security pins, also add a second layer of authentication when logging into an account. Secure websites will often ask for certain characters of a passcode, for instance the 2nd and 5th letters, etc. before allowing access.

- An **SMS message** containing a security PIN is an increasingly common form of multi-factor authentication. The biggest privacy concern with this is the need to share a mobile phone number with the website provider. A security concern is many SMS messages are sent unencrypted and can be intercepted or stolen by specifically targeted mobile malware.

- Several **biometric methods** can also be used. These would include fingerprint scanners, iris scans, and facial recognition apps.

- Secured **authenticator mobile apps** are becoming more commonly used. The app generates a second code, which is displayed on the mobile phone.

Numerous sites now offer multi-factor authentication including: Online backup, banking, cryptocurrency, email, gaming, and many social media sites including Facebook, Twitter, LinkedIn, and Google+.

Most sites offer multi-factor authentication as an option. However, as a convenience to users it's not always enabled by default. This is unfortunate as relying on a simple password is not a good security option. It's highly recommended that you enable multi-factor authentication where it's offered.

For a complete list of sites offering multi-factor authentication, take a look at the very useful Two-Factor Authentication website https://twofactorauth.org

Biometrics is another fast growing, access control technology that can provide additional security to devices and applications. As the adoption of biometrics as a form of identity verification increases, many are predicting the demise of numeric (knowledge based) passwords. You literally become the password. Multi-factor biometric access solutions combining passwords and a biometric form of identity are extremely effective and a secure form of access control.

There are numerous biometric solutions available that can either be used on their own or in conjunction with other access control solutions to provide multi-factor authentication access.

Examples include:

- Facial recognition
- Fingerprint scanning technology
- Iris scan
- Palm vein scanners
- Voice recognition

Facial recognition applications can be used to authenticate the identity of a user instead of or in conjunction with a numeric password. Android phones (starting from 4.1) offer facial recognition as a method to unlock your phone.

Some facial recognition systems require the user to blink to "prove" they are alive and not a photo being used to gain access. The important issue apart from ease of use is how well the system handles privacy. Who has control over and owns the user access images? Also an important question is where do the images reside? On the user's device in an encrypted form is good; being uploaded to the vendor's site is bad.

- **Sensible Vision** (http://www.sensiblevision.com) is an example of a product that allows users to own their image and stores the images used for access control as an encrypted file on their own device.

Fingerprint scanning technology can be seen in numerous devices. Apple introduced a fingerprint sensor in its iPhone 5S (TouchID) to replace or complement using a password.

- **StickyPassword** password manager (https://www.stickypassword.com) adds fingerprint scanning to authenticate user access to multiple apps. Smart idea!

Iris scanners capture the unique shape of the iris using mathematical pattern recognition. Just as with other biometric markers, we all have unique shaped irises. Well loved in sci-fi films, a criticism of iris scanning however is a high definition photo of an eye can fool them. Hackers in Germany have demonstrated how they can recreate an image of an iris from a photo. This isn't stopping national governments, many of which love biometric systems like iris scanners, as they are deployed as part of large national ID systems.

Another criticism has been the range of iris scanners. Researchers at Carnegie Mellon University have developed a high-resolution camera that is capable of scanning an iris at a distance of 40 feet. So expect to see more of these systems soon.

Palm vein scanners use infrared light to capture and digitalize the unique patterns of veins in the skin beneath the palm. It is similar to a fingerprint scanner, except contact is not required. The user places their hand over the reader, which then compares the reading to the previously captured digital image for authentication.

Palm readers are being deployed in schools, hospitals, at ATMs, and for retail checkouts. They are currently being integrated into numerous login systems to provide strong user authentication. As prices come down, you can expect to see palm vein scanners integrated into multiple new devices. Expect to see palm readers in numerous IoT applications *(see Internet-of-Things for more details)*.

Voice recognition works like most biometric applications by capturing a sample and comparing the voiceprint to grant access. We all have unique voice signatures so voice recognition is starting to make its way into mobile solutions as a form of authentication.

Passwords and Access Control: Take Action Steps

Password managers are highly recommended to create and manage all your passwords. If possible add multi-factor authentication to strengthen the solution. Password manger solutions I like include:

- **LastPass** (https://lastpass.com). One of the leading password managers. LastPass works with most browsers and operating systems. LastPass also has numerous ways to add multi-factor authentication, which is highly recommended. The premium edition will sync passwords across multiple devices.

- **StickyPassword** (www.stickypassword.com). This password manager adds two-factor biometric authentication with fingerprint scanning.

- **KeePass** (www.keepass.info). This is a highly rated open-source alternative password manager. KeePass is portable and can be saved to and run from a USB drive.

Simple programing errors are often responsible for major failures. Programing flaws and errors are commonly referred to as bugs. In browsers, media players, email programs, and other applications, bugs are constantly being discovered. Once an application bug is uncovered, software vendors may develop and issue a patch or wait until a planned upgrade is released. The action depends on the severity or security vulnerability caused by the uncovered bug.

Unpatched software applications are one of the most serious online cyber security risks that leave devices vulnerable to attack online. Your system can be infected just by visiting a website where there is a ready-made malware exploit. The malware is waiting to take advantage of unpatched plug-ins and common applications. This often occurs in the background without the user's knowledge. Users get tricked into visiting exploited sites by email and social media phishing campaigns.

An indication of how widespread this problem is came to light recently after the occurrence of a massive breach of computer records from the U.S. Government Office of Personnel Management (OPM). (4.2 million Federal personnel files were stolen in early 2015 in the largest ever theft of U.S. government documents.) After the attacks and during an investigation of Federal government systems, it was discovered that there were nearly 3,000 critical and high-risk unpatched vulnerabilities. These were found in the computer systems of three different bureaus of the U.S. Department of the Interior. Any of these unpatched systems could have been exploited by attackers, allowing access to Federal systems like the ones that ended up being hacked.[68]

Bug Bounty Gold Rush
In response to breaches caused by software errors, most software development vendors, as well as many online businesses and websites, have developed so-called "bug

bounty" programs. These offer rewards and recognition to researchers and hackers who find and report software bugs.[69] This has led to a gold rush of computer programmers combing through software application code hoping to cash in by discovering new errors.

In an illustration of the number of flaws and vulnerabilities there actually are in modern software programs, consider Yahoo's bug bounty program. In the last two years, 10,000 submissions were made. Of these, 1,500 resulted in payments made to researchers. Thus indicating Yahoo had at least 1,500 flaws in their software and websites. In total they paid out over $1 million to the researchers.[70] Looking at the bigger picture, $1 million is a small amount of money to stop malicious hackers from taking advantage of unpatched vulnerabilities.

It's not only legitimate software development companies who are interested in acquiring newly discovered software bugs. The criminal underground and many white-hat hackers will pay handsomely for any new unpatched bug. Especially if the bug causes a vulnerability that will allow them access to user's systems and bypass installed security products. Criminal hacker groups have been known to pay tens and even hundreds of thousands of dollars to purchase serious zero-day (previously unknown) exploits.

National intelligence and law enforcement agencies are also direct buyers of newly discovered software bugs. Especially if they can lead to the development of a zero-day exploit allowing them to hack individual targets of interest to them. This is leading to a shadowy industry where bug and exploit buying firms aim to outbid vendors in an attempt to get their hands on valuable zero-day exploits. For example, Zerodium, a high-end bug buying company (they only buy exploitable zero-day bugs), tweeted that Google had paid $1,337 for the recent Android Stagefright bug. Zerodium claimed they would have paid $100,000 for it.[71] This upping of the ante will only lead to more dangerous exploits ending up in the hands of government agencies and criminal syndicates.

They are prepared to splash out huge amounts of money because of the potential returns they can make from the exploits.

Patching the Holes

The average PC user in the United States has 76 programs installed with at least 27 different update mechanisms needed to keep them patched and secure. It's no wonder that many hackers focus on exploiting unpatched applications to infect user's systems. Unpatched applications include operating systems, browsers, and applications of all kinds on PCs, smartphones, tablets, and other devices.

The more common the application, the bigger the potential market for hackers to pursue with focused attention. (This is the main reason it's important to pay attention to all browser and operating system updates, and to patch them as soon as updates are available.)

The same applies to company computers. According to the IBM X-Force 2015 security research team, [72] hackers compromised at least one billion records containing personally identifiable information (PII) in 2014. The researchers highlighted software vulnerabilities (mostly unpatched systems) as one of the largest contributing factors. Other key findings were:

- There were update patches available for 83% of all vulnerabilities on the day they become publicly known, so it is possible to remediate the majority of vulnerabilities, as they become known. However, those who got hacked had failed to install the updated patches.

- 5% of the average users installed applications are end-of-life programs that are no longer patched by the vendor. These should be removed or replaced as they can be a security risk.

- The leading three most exposed programs (based on their prominence and how many users have neglected to patch them) were:

  ○ 1st **Oracle JRE 1.7.x/7.x** was unpatched on 77% of user's machines, even though 101 vulnerabilities were detected in the program over the past year. *(Java and JavaScript are two totally different products. You need JavaScript but probably not Java, so it makes sense to uninstall it.)*

  ○ 2nd **Apple QuickTime 7.x**, *which* was unpatched on 37% of machines.

  ○ 3rd **Adobe Reader x 10.x**, which was unpatched on 65% of machines.

Although not in the top 3 unpatched programs of 2015, **Adobe Flash Player** bears special mention. It is often referred to as the "Internet's screen door" due to having so many holes. Flash Player is a favorite with hackers due to the high number of individual unpatched systems and so many undocumented security vulnerabilities in the product. Recently, the situation has become so bad that many are calling for Adobe to end-of-life the product. It should go without saying that you need to update and patch Adobe Flash player as soon as updates become available.

System Updates: Take Action Steps

Microsoft Windows Systems

To have Windows automatically download and install important upgrades, enable automatic updates.

- "Settings," click "Change PC settings," "Update and recovery," click "Choose how updates get installed" and under "Important updates," choose install automatically.

Apple Macintosh Systems

Apple Macintosh users can install OS X updates automatically when the updates become available through the App Store:

- In OS X 10.10 Yosemite click "Turn On" in the Turn on Always Update? Notification when a new update is announced for the first time. Alternatively, enable automatic updates in App Store preferences: From the Apple menu, choose "System Preferences." Click "App Store."

Apple iOS—iPhones and iPads

Apple iOS users are able to update iPhones and iPads wirelessly or via iTunes. Updating iOS on Apple devices is a simple task. As Apple produces its own phones, there are a limited number of iPhone and iPad versions per generation. This simplifies the whole issue of updating.

Apple sends out update notices when a new update is ready. It's advisable to backup all data before conducting the update. Simply follow the onscreen instruction to update wirelessly.

Android phones and tablets

As of November 2015, "Marshmallow" 6.0 is the latest version of Android. Android 4.4 "Kitkat" is the most widely used version, found on 39.2% of devices accessing Google Play. At least 50% of Android devices are still using versions ranging from 2.3 "Gingerbread" (which was first available on devices in 2011) to version 4.3 "Jellybean" (first available in late 2013).

The above numbers indicate what most of us know, updating Android devices is messy and can be complicated or even impossible on some phones. Android is sold to numerous phone and tablet hardware vendors who all add their custom drivers, software, and hardware features. This open eco-system makes it difficult for Google to control how updates are released to the public. Hardware manufacturers have to update their software to ensure they work with the latest release of

Android OS. Some lower end phones are never updated if they don't have enough RAM to support the new version of Android. Additionally, phone vendors and carriers would rather sell newer phones than update old software.

To update the version of Android on a phone, use the following settings:
- Open "Setting Application."
- Go to "About device" and choose, "Software update."
- Click on "Update" to check if there is an update available. If there is, start the update.

Android users can select to receive app auto-updates in their Google Play settings. You are able to select automatic updates per app or for all:
- Tap on "Menu" and go to "Settings." Check the "Auto-update apps" option. Choose the apps you want to update automatically. Apps will now update without the need for user interaction.

Application Updates: Take Action Steps

Adobe, in an effort to keep **Flash Player** secure, releases patches monthly and often sends out emergency fixes in-between. It's vitally important to keep Abode Flash Player updated, so if you get notification of an update, install it straight away.

In the meantime, to check if you are running the latest Adobe Flash version and updates, use this link:

- http://www.adobe.com/software/flash/about/
  A list of browsers and the latest updates available for each are listed, plus what you have installed. (If you have Flash blocked, enable it to check what version you have installed). If you don't have the

current update for your browser, install it right away.

Alternatively, you can totally remove Adobe Flash Player from your device. (This option will not be so popular with young adults and teens!) Sure there might be a few videos you won't be able to view, but you will have a far more secure system. In many browsers, you can disable Flash, in the Plug-in settings and simply re-enable it if/when you really need it.

Java is another browser plug-in that needs to be kept updated. Java normally checks for updates and alerts you when any are ready to be installed. However, if the program has been disabled, to check you have the latest releases you can check manually:

• Open www.java.com in a new window. Click the link that says, "Do I have Java?" If your system does have Java installed, click "Verify Java version." You will either have no Java installed or it's disabled, or your version is outdated, if so update it.

For more technically advanced users, **NoScript** (https://noscript.net) is a free, open source FireFox extension used to block Flash content (as well as Java, Java script, Flashlight and other plug-ins). This lets you keep them installed and controls when they run. I don't normally recommend NoScript to everyone as it can take some getting used to. But it's really not difficult to use, and it forces you think about what scripts to allow. (Note: There are several simple and easy to follow NoScript tutorial videos on YouTube. These will quickly explain NoScript. Go watch it and then you can download NoScript.)

You need to keep other **non-Microsoft applications running on Windows** based systems updated. For this there are two useful and free applications that you can use and choose from:

- **Secunia PSI**—Personal Software Inspector (https://secunia.com) supports all versions of Windows from XP to 8.1

Secunia PSI scans for unpatched applications and automatically updates them. If a program can't be updated, Secunia will inform you and give instructions on how to get updated. In addition, another useful feature is that it detects and lists end-of-life programs that are unsecure with no available patches. These should be removed or replaced.

- **Patch My PC** application (http://www.patchmypc.net) monitors over a hundred common Windows applications for updates and installs patches. (Including numerous browsers, Adobe Flash Player, Java, GIMP, OpenOffice and others). Patch My PC can be saved to and run from a USB drive if you want to check and patch applications on numerous devices.

Anti-malware

As discussed in Chapter 6, malicious malware is an ever present and growing threat online.

False Sense of Security
Over-reliance on anti-malware software gives a false sense of security to millions of computer users everywhere. As mentioned previously, no anti-malware software will ever keep your system 100% secure. So while there are numerous, well-established anti-malware companies, whose products I do recommend, they are part (an important part) of the solution to securing your data and ultimately your privacy.

Just to re-state, I believe anti-malware is useful and recommended. Everyone should install premium, paid for anti-malware on his or her devices. However, understand anti-malware is not a silver bullet and may only catch 50% to 90% of malware at the most. (Estimates vary regarding the effectiveness of anti-malware products.) If you happen to be one of the first to get hit by new malware before the anti-malware vendors have updated their software, your system will be infected.

Just to put the issue of the effectiveness of anti-malware products into perspective, remember according to AVTest they see approximately 390,000 pieces of malware every day.[73] Malware writers know they have on average between 5 to 30 days or more before all the major vendors have updated their systems against their newly released malware.[74] So as a user it all depends when you come across a particular malware exploit and if your system does or does not recognize it.

Multi-license Management Console

If you are the computer go-to-person for your family or small company, most anti-malware products have an online management console that allows you to see the condition of the protected devices. In my family and office I can see all the devices where I have installed anti-malware; when they were last scanned and any issues with their protection. This is especially useful if you have teenagers (who are online all the time) or less technically aware members of your tribe. It's a quick way to check if their anti-malware is up to date without having to visit each device.

Apple Mac

A surprising number of Macintosh users erroneously believe they are immune to malware attacks. This is totally incorrect and puts them at risk. As Macs have become more popular, so malware writers have started to focus more of their attention on them. It's also not only the fact that Macs are an ever-growing market, but also who is using them. Many senior managers and executives use them both at work and at home. This is an attractive demographic for cyber criminals to target. Plus most Mac users don't install anti-malware, making them a softer target.

136

It's correct that there are almost no Mac viruses, and far less Mac OS X malware than for Windows. However, this is changing. In 2015 there has been 5 times more Apple malware than the 5 previous years combined.[75] We have also seen proof-of-concept Apple OS X malware that will allow unsigned code to run on your Macintosh.

There are also trojans that affect Macs users if they are tricked into installing them. For example, in early 2012 a Java vulnerability in Mac OS X allowed the Flashback trojan to infect over 600,000 Apple Mac computers in a successful drive-by download attack. Although within a number of weeks there were fixes for Java, many simply disabled Java altogether. Two years after Flashback first appeared, in mid-2014 it was estimated by security researchers that there were still over 20,000 Apple Macs infected with the trojan. Shellshock also affected Macs as did the Browlock trojan.

Mobile malware is a growing problem, and too many users are still oblivious to it. Fortunately there are numerous mobile anti-malware solutions available. (*See Chapter nine for details on protecting mobile devices.*)

Anti-malware: Take Action Steps

Microsoft Windows is still the dominant desktop operating system installed worldwide. As such, malware writers have targeted their wares at Microsoft based systems for years.

While many users and even technicians have favorites, there are numerous established Windows based anti-malware vendors you can choose from including:

- **Webroot, Norton (Symantec), F-Secure, Trend-Micro, Sophos, McAfee (Intel), Avast, Eset** and others. All have well-established Windows based solutions with products aimed at consumers, small and medium businesses and enterprises.

o   Note, I no longer recommend **AVG** due to the company's practice of selling its user's information to advertisers.

For **Mac** users, there are a handful of OS X anti-malware protection solutions available. Below are two I like. Both are free products and work well:

- **Avast Mac Security**
(https://www.avast.com/free-mac-security), this product scored 100% detection of malware in both the AV-Test (April 2015) and on the AV-Comparatives test.[76]

- **Avira** (http://www.avira.com), free anti-virus for Mac, which constantly scores well in both AV-Test & AV Comparatives independent anti-virus researcher testing.

Firewalls

A firewall is a first line of defense device that filters data before it enters your private network. For businesses, any Internet connection should be protected by a hardware firewall. At home your WiFi router that's connected to the Internet has a built-in firewall.

In simple terms, a firewall is designed to reject any network traffic that does not link to a request from inside the network. So it stops packets of data you didn't request from entering your network. Hardware firewalls are configured via a web-based interface from inside the network.

All modern operating systems include a software firewall, as do many high-end anti-malware packages.

To enable the Windows and Apple Mac built-in firewalls:

Windows 7: To turn on the firewall: Click the "Start button," click "Control panel," search for "firewall" and click "Windows firewall." Click to turn the firewall on.

Windows 8: To turn on the firewall. Go to the "Control panel," choose "Systems & Security," then "Windows Firewall" if not enabled, and click "Turn on Windows firewall" for all networks listed.

Windows 10: The firewall is tuned on by default. If it has been disabled for any reason, go to "Settings," "Update & Security," select "Windows Firewall" and turn it back on.

Apple Mac: To enable the built-in firewall, open "System preferences," select the "Security & Privacy" icon. Click on the "Firewall" tab. If it's not marked on, click on the padlock in the lower left corner to make a change to the setting. Click "on."

At the same time, under "advanced options" check the following:

- "Enable stealth mode"—this will stop your Mac from responding to outside attempts to contact it.
- "Automatically allow signed software to receive incoming connections."

Don't check "Block all incoming connections." This is the most secure option, but can cause some applications to stop working. Rather allow the applications like Skype, etc. that need to respond to be listed. If you see any applications you don't recognize, disable them by choosing the "block incoming connections" option.

When you have done this, click OK to exit, and relock the setting to save your changes.

Encrypting your data is probably the single most important action you can take to secure it from unauthorized viewing.

Encryption is the process of taking plaintext (a message or data file), combining it with a randomly generated key and mixing them together using a mathematical operation. The result is a scrambled text (referred to as a ciphertext) that can only be read once it is decrypted. A decryption key is applied to unencrypt the ciphertext back into readable plain text again.

Encrypting your data files is one of the most effective means of protection. It is invaluable if your device, removable drive, or system is stolen, hacked, or accessed without your permission. Unless the hacker or thief has the password to unencrypt your data files, good luck to them! Most commercial encryption is enough to stump the vast majority of hackers. Unless they can guess or recover your password, your encrypted data will be useless to them. *(See Password section regards setting secure passwords.)*

Mobile devices are often lost or stolen. So if you use a laptop or mobile device of any kind, data encryption is essential to protect sensitive documents. We have all heard the stories about company executives leaving laptops on planes, trains, and in taxis. If the device is encrypted this will, in the vast majority of cases, prevent sensitive and personal data from being accessed and stolen. As mentioned several times, no system is ever 100% secure. Although rare, it is possible for really skilled hackers to successfully attack encrypted drives if they have access to the psychical device, the correct forensic tools, enough time and know-how. However, in the vast majority of cases, encryption is good enough to prevent unauthorized access to your data.

Encrypting your data files is equally important if you are using or planning to store any data in a cloud service of any kind. If the systems of the cloud provider are breached, again your data needs to be encrypted to ensure it remains uncompromised and can't be accessed your password and/or other user authentication.

Data Encryption Options

There are two basic options when encrypting data. Full disk encryption programs encrypt all the contents of a drive while file level encryption allows for the encryption of individual files or folders.

Microsoft Windows Encryption

Users of Microsoft Windows have several choices regarding encryption.

The easiest choice is to use **BitLocker**, which is Microsoft's native encryption product. It's available with the Ultimate and Professional editions of Windows Vista and 7 or the Professional or Enterprise editions of Windows 8, 8.1, or 10. BitLocker is a full disk encryption solution that uses AES encryption (BitLocker Drive encryption) and removable drives (BitLocker To Go).

BitLocker is available to use in 3 different modes:

- Transparent mode, which requires the computer to have a Trusted Platform Module (TPM) crypto processor chip. (Found in most premium or business laptops and tablets.) The keys required for encryption are locked in the TPM chip. The user logs in as normal.

- User authentication mode. The user requires a PIN to login.

- USB Key mode. Windows login requires a USB device, which contains the startup key. This is the most secure option as the USB is used as a security token to authenticate the user.

When using BitLocker, as with most encryption technologies, it's important to make a copy of your unlock key. Without a copy you could be locked out of your system if you forget your password. (Best option is to keep a copy on a USB drive or a print out.) Windows 8 also offers the option of saving your unlock key to OneDrive. (This is not something I would recommend, but you can do this if you are concerned about misplacing other copies.)

If you are one of the many millions of Windows Vista, 7 or 8 Home or Core users who don't have Bitlocker built-into the systems, here are some alternative encryption products for Windows:

- **BestCrypt,** which is from Finnish company, Jetico (www.jetico.com). BestCrypt volume encryption is a full disk encryption solution. It has extensive options including support for encryption keys on hardware tokens. Plus they also support Windows XP (if you still haven't upgraded which I recommend you do).
- If you work with multiple types of systems, such as Windows, Mac OS, and Linux, a really good feature is the encrypted containers, which allow the seamless movement of encrypted files between devices.
- If you would prefer an open-source solution that works well for all MS Windows systems, look at **DiskCryptor** (www.diskcryptor.net), or **VeraCrypt** (https://veracrypt.codeplex.com), which is based on but not compatible with TrueCrypt.

I would no longer suggest long-time favorite **TrueCrypt** as the product has been abandoned. An announcement was posted on the TrueCrypt website in May 2014, stating that the product was no longer secure (or at least that it contained unfixed security issues). They recommended that users should look for alternatives to encrypt their data.[77] Much speculation surrounds the announcement. Whatever the reason, and despite some security researchers still promoting the product, I would recommend one of the alternatives already mentioned. If your drives are already secured with TrueCrypt, you should migrate the data from them.

Apple Mac Encryption

Full Disk Encryption

Mac OS X comes with FileVault, built-in full disk encryption. You can encrypt your entire Mac drive plus any removable drives with FileVault.

FileVault works on the fly, encrypting new data as it's saved and unencrypting it as it's retrieved. It uses XTS-AES 128 encryption, which is strong enough for most users.

A password is required to access your files. When you first encrypt your disk, a 24-character alphanumeric recovery key is provided. It's vital to record this somewhere safe in case you forget your password. Apple provides the option of storing the recovery key with them. If you choose this option you have to answer several additional security questions. Apple states that if you don't give the exact answers, you won't be able to obtain your security key from them. So for anyone who goes this route, write down the answers and store them in a very safe place.

File Encryption

If you don't want to encrypt your entire hard drive, using FileVault, it's possible to create a disk image and save individual files or entire directories to it, which will be automatically encrypted.

Encryption: Take Action Steps

Install one of the solutions recommended above and encrypt your data!

- No encryption will do any good if you protect it with a weak password. *(See section on Passwords and Access control earlier in this chapter.)*

Backups

Regular data backups are an essential part of keeping your data secure. If a disaster wipes out your hard drive, your backup files are your lifeline to restoring your data, photos, music, and videos.

With the proliferation of smartphones and tablets, it's easy to forget how much data we all capture and keep on them. Mobile devices are often at more risk of losing data due to loss of the device or destruction, like dropping your mobile phone into water!

Malware is another major cause of data loss. A ransomware encrypted device can certainly wipe out all of your data unless you have current backups.

Don't forget to backup your data and protect your personal photos and videos when your computer has to be worked on by a technician. It's best to backup all photos (and personal data), and delete the originals on your device before sending it in for repairs or upgrades of any kind. It's definitely creepy, and I'm sure not all computer repair technicians are stalkers (I know many with a high standard of ethics and integrity). But there have been numerous cases where repair technicians have received a computer to work on and have immediately viewed the photos and data on the device. They have even copied information off devices for later viewing! So it's best to protect yourself and your privacy. The same advice applies to your mobile phone and tablet.

Backup Devices and Services

USB drives are cheap and useful for quick backups. They are however easy to steal or lose. For that reason, always encrypt the data on all your USB drives.

There are lots of available **portable external storage devices** to choose from. Add encryption and you are ready to start backing up. *(See section on Encryption for more details.)*

If you use a **cloud based back service**, a zero-knowledge solution is the only way to go. While all cloud storage vendors make claims about the security of your data, they don't tell the whole story. Yes, they may encrypt your data on their servers, but they hold the encryption keys. This means if for any reason, they wish to read anything or hand your data over to anyone else, they can do so, all without your knowledge. This is a major weakness of most cloud-based systems.

A **zero-knowledge service** is different because you—and only you—the owner of the data has access to your files. You hold the encryption keys. If you lose the keys and don't have a backup, no one including the cloud backup service provider or any other technology firm can help you. In security and privacy terms that's a good thing. It effectively means that the cloud service provider has no way to access your data. If they did, all they would see are scrambled chucks of encrypted data that make no sense without your keys. It also means if they are ever hacked, your data would be useless to anyone who may steal or copy it. Lastly, even if any government agency wanted to view your data, there is no way the cloud vendor could give them access, as only you hold the keys. That's a zero-knowledge system and it's the most secure type of cloud service available.

Like all security solutions you need to understand their strengths and weaknesses. Zero-knowledge cloud backup solutions are secure when used correctly. They encrypt your data on your system (client side encryption), upload it and only unencrypt it again when you download it from the cloud.

The weak point is your password. Adding multi-factor authentication is advisable.

Backup software makes regular incremental backing up easier. *(See Backups: Take Action Steps for more details.)*

Backup Strategy

Most businesses follow the 3-2-1 rule of backing up data. Three copies on at least two different media types with one copy being offsite (in the cloud). There's nothing wrong with anyone applying that advice to their personal data as well. I personally use several USD drives, two portable backup devices, and a cloud based service. *(See Backups: Take Action Steps for details.)*

In order to decide which files (such as data, images, videos, recordings etc.) to store where and how often to back them up, it's best to review your data as follows:

- Identify your most critical files and make securing copies a priority. This is any financial data, current working documents, copies of important documents, family photos and videos. All these need to be on an encrypted portable drive and backed up at least weekly. Any new files should be backed up daily to your encrypted USB drive.

- Identify which files contain sensitive account and financial data. If any contain personal identifiable information, put those on a zero-knowledge, cloud based backup server. Or if you are really cautious you might want to skip the cloud-based service for this data altogether. For non-zero-knowledge cloud storage, personally I would only use this service for something that I would not mind seeing posted somewhere. For example, non-personal photos taken at a public or sports event, or documents that are already on the Internet on social media, etc.

Files you might want to share with a group, but certainly nothing confidential or private.

- Burn to DVD any photo, video and music files that don't change very often. Old family photos, music, holiday videos, etc. that can't be replaced. Keep the copies in a safe place (a waterproof/fireproof safe is good).

Backups: Take Action Steps

Keep your backup strategy simple:
- Copy all photos, notes and videos from your phone and cameras to your laptop. Incorporate them into your file systems and save them.

- **Incremental backups**: Use backup software to make incremental backups of important documents to an attached portable drive. All backups should be encrypted.

- **Daily backups**: Backup current files and documents in progress onto an encrypted USB drive daily. If you are working on something of importance (such as writing a report, or book, etc.) backup more often.

(I keep the USB disconnected from my laptop unless I'm busy backing up documents. The reason for keeping this daily backup device unattached is simple. If my system were to get infected by something like ransomware, which would probably encrypt the device and all mapped drives, the air gap will save my daily backups from being infected. Maybe paranoid I know, but it's secure!)

- **Full backup:** Do a complete backup weekly to an encrypted external drive. Keep this removable drive disconnected from your laptop when you are not backing up documents. Set up schedule reminders so you don't miss the weekly backup.

- **Cloud based storage:** You can use occasional cloud backup for non-critical files and photos. No PII should ever be sent to a cloud system. It's a good practice to encrypt all files before uploading to a cloud service.

Backup Products I Like
There are numerous backup solutions available so I don't really have any hard and fast recommendations. Just find something you can use and make certain you follow a regular backup routine. That's the key to not losing data if your device is lost or becomes corrupted.

- **IronKey** (http://ironkey.com) and **Apricorn** (http://www.apricorn.com) both have robust, ready to go ranges of encrypted USB and removable backup devices.

There are lots of good backup software products on the market. Picking a product you like and using it to make incremental backups is the key. Solutions I like include:

- **Backup Maker** (https://www.ascomp.de/en/) is available for all versions of Microsoft Windows.

- **Genie9** (http://www.genie9.com)

- **ChronoSync** (http://www.econtechnologies.com) to backup and synchronize data on Apple devices.

- Although not a zero-knowledge backup solution, **CrashPlan** https://www.code42.com/crashplan/ is a good choice for individuals, families, small businesses as well as enterprises to backup general data. CrashPlan has good security features and offers automatic incremental and differential back-ups to local drives, offsite drives or cloud storage.

Zero-knowledge, secure cloud-based backup vendors to consider include:

- **Tresorit** (https://tresorit.com) is a Swiss based, zero-knowledge, secure cloud based backup service. Tresorit has a robust admin center, which makes it suitable to manage multiple devices or to use in a business setting. They offer true zero-knowledge access for all desktop and mobile clients. All the data that is uploaded to their servers is encrypted before it leaves your device.

- **SpiderOak** (https://spideroak.com) is a U.S. based, zero-knowledge encrypted cloud based backup solution. It needs to be pointed out that zero-knowledge ONLY applies when their desktop client is used (encrypt the files on your desktop and upload them). However, at the time of writing this does not apply when using the mobile app or web-based access.
  - Source—SpiderOak Android app login screen: Not zero-knowledge. If you login with this mobile client, or via the website, your password will exist in the SpiderOak server memory during your browsing session. If you prefer to use only zero-knowledge access, cancel this login, and only login via the SpiderOak desktop client, which is more secure.

Deleting Old Files

Whenever you dispose of an old system (computer, backup device, tablet, or phone) it's important to ensure permanent deletion of sensitive files and data. If not you could risk discovery of your data by a computer technician, snoop, criminal, or just anyone who acquires your discarded device.

If you are using Microsoft Windows, simply dragging a file on your desktop to the trash bin is not deleting it. You have only removed the links to where the file can still be found. Until they are overwritten by new data the files are still there.

On traditional mechanical hard drives, USB flash drives, SD cards, and external solid-state drives (SSD) many "deleted" files are relatively easy to recover using simple file recovery software tools. Recovery programs can find the raw data even after a quick disk format. Private and sensitive data including passwords, financials or health records, photos and personal emails can all be exposed if not permanently erased.

The exception is when using internal solid-state drives. When files are deleted on a modern internal SSD, the operating system sends a TRIM command to immediately wipe the blocks of data where the file was saved. Thus it's almost impossible to recover deleted files from an internal SSD. However, it doesn't apply to external SSD devices. TRIM doesn't work over USB or FireWire interfaces, meaning the files on them are just as vulnerable to those on older mechanical hard drives.

To protect all files (deleted or not) on removable media, USB drives, external backup drives, etc., encrypt the files. If you ever lose the drive or it's stolen, your data will still be safe. (*See section on Encryption for more details.*)

Deleting Files: Take Action Steps

To securely delete data, you need to overwrite the file, scramble the file and folder data, and remove the file from the Shadow Copy/Restore points to make sure that any of the file traces are securely deleted.

Ensuring that data files have been overwritten 7 times meets the U.S. Department of Defense 5220-22-M standard for secure file deletion.

Microsoft Windows secure file deletion solutions:
Like millions of other users, for many years I have used **CCleaner** (www.piriform.com/ccleaner). It is useful to clean up old Internet files, Windows files, and temporary files as well as removing cookies, recent documents, and more. There is a limited free product that does a good job. There is also a paid for professional edition which offers support and automatic updates. CCleaner has the option to overwrite files 1, 7, or 35 times. Seven should be enough for anyone reading this book.

Apple Macintosh users have a built-in solution to permanently erase files. Drag the files sent to the trashcan icon. In the Finder view, go to "Finder Preferences." Under the "Advanced tab" check "Empty Trash securely." This overwrites the disk space with a series of 7 different passes in which random information is written to the disk sectors previously occupied by that file. Apple states that this secure erasure meets United States Department of Defense security standards.

Secure Email

Email is still the way the world communicates. Over 4 billion people worldwide have email accounts.[78] In 2014 an estimated 182.9 billion emails per day were sent and received globally.

Protecting your personal email account is more important than most people realize. It's not just the content of personal emails, but in many cases your email account is used to authenticate your access to numerous online services, accounts, and social media sites. So if your email account is broken into, the smart hacker will look through your emails. They will search for any password reset emails (which should always be deleted after use) or messages from your bank, PayPal, iTunes, Dropbox, and other online accounts and services. Then they will head straight to those online services and try to login using the same password/email combinations they now know or will use simple variations. In many cases they are successful.

In addition to being a gateway to many other online services, email accounts usually hold a lot of personal and private information that can be used to commit identity theft by anyone who can gain access.

Notorious convicted Romanian hacker Marcel Lazer, aka, "Guccifer," is currently serving prison time for breaking into numerous high-profile email accounts. He puts it like this, "Emails are full of secrets, that's the place to find them." He should know—he successfully hacked the emails (and social media accounts) of dozens of high-profile people. Some of his victims are American politicians and business leaders, including those close to former President George W. Bush, Hillary Clinton, a former member of the U.S. Joint Chiefs of Staff, Presidential advisors, members of the Rockefeller family, and board members of the Federal Reserve Bank. Lazer guessed the answers to security questions (easy if they are all over social media or on Wikipedia) for the email accounts in order to gain access. Once he had accessed the email and social media accounts, Lazer leaked personal photos and other details he stole online.[79]

Today it's not even necessary to have technical skills to break into someone's email account. New York City private investigator Eric Saldarriaga simply went online and hired hackers in order to steal the email usernames and passwords of people he was investigating. Likewise, Saldarriaga did the same to individuals he wasn't actually investigating but were of interest to him. However, Saldarriaga wasn't as smart as he thought he was and is currently serving time in prison for his hacking crimes.[80]

Both of these, plus numerous other examples, clearly demonstrate the need for taking email security seriously.

You need more Email Accounts

One of the first email strategies to implement is to separate your business from personal emails. Never mix the two. That way if you lose an account you limit the damage. By adding an additional email account that is used just for social media sites, you further segment your emails and add more protection. If one of your accounts gets hacked, you won't lose everything.

Encrypting Email Content

If you would like to keep your emails private and stop anyone from reading them (including your email provider), encryption is the only route to go. If you don't use encryption, you need to consider the fact that writing email is easily read by outside eyes, because that's what can happen.

Unless your email is encrypted it is probably being read by machines (looking for keywords) and can be read by individuals at various junctions. If any of the victims of Saldarriaga or Guccifer had used encryption in their email system, even though the hackers might have been able to access their accounts, they wouldn't have been able to read the encrypted contents without the corresponding keys required for decryption.

Note, when using email encryption the content of the email and attachments are encrypted. However, the subject line is not, so don't type anything confidential there.

Using Email Encryption

OpenPGP (Pretty Good Privacy) is a form of public-key encryption. In order to use it you have to generate a key pair—a public and private key. These are really just big chunks of random letters and numbers used to scramble and unscramble your data messages. You always keep the private key private and you openly share the public key.

- Public key—can and should be available to anyone so they can encrypt and send messages to you.

- Private key—stored securely and protected by a password. Used to decrypt messages sent to you.

So anyone who wants to communicate securely with you uses your public key to scramble (encrypt) a message. Once you receive the message, you use your private key to unscramble the text. An additional use of the private key is to sign and send emails. The private key proves you sent the message.

Anytime you create a PGP key pair, make sure you keep a backup in a secure location (such as on an encrypted USB drive), and don't lose your password. Most PGP email services do not have any type of key recovery service. So if you lose your password or your private key, you are out of luck—there is no way to recover any encrypted messages. If a service offers key recovery, it's not really secure at all! If the company can unlock your messages, who else has access to them?

OpenPGP is open-source so the source code has been vetted and tested by lots of people as being secure.

A quick note regarding encryption names. People will often use different terms for the same thing when discussing encryption—GnuPG, GPG, GNU Privacy Guard, Open PGP, and PGP are all used interchangeably. OpenPGP (Pretty Good Privacy) is the encryption standard. GNU PrivacyGuard, which can be shortened to GPG or GnuPG, are programs used to implement the encryption. If this is hard to grasp, don't worry, you aren't required to know exactly how all the pieces hang together to use encryption. It works very well when used correctly in your email and it's really easier to use than to explain!

A useful site to lookup public PGP keys is Keybase (https://keybase.io). You can run a search by using a person's social media name from Twitter, GitHub, Reddit, and/or Coinbase to see if they have a public PGP key to communicate with.

Webmail Clients

For those with webmail accounts such as Gmail, Yahoo, GMX, or Outlook webmail, there are several browser plug-in encryption products like Secure Gmail and Mailvelope.

Desktop Mail Clients

If you are using a desktop email client like Mozilla Thunderbird or Postbox, you will need to add GnuPG, a free implantation of OpenPGP and Enigmail (an Open PGP add-on that works with both desktop clients).

Privacy focused, Encrypted Email Services

In the wake of the Edward Snowden leaks, the two leading U.S. based encrypted email companies—Lavabit and Silent Circle, both closed their doors rather than hand their client emails over to the NSA. Since then several new start-ups, all based outside the USA have set up shop to fill the privacy based email space. They all offer different degrees of anonymity and privacy.

For those who are more interested in a private encrypted email option, there are several non-U.S. based offerings listed in the Take Action Steps section below. The big selling point for most is that they are not located in the USA. So they will not be subject to any requests for data from the NSA. Rather they are protected by stronger privacy legislation outside of both the U.S. and the European Union (EU) and are not subject to the Patriot Act. If that's important to you, then there are several to choose from.

Secure Email: Take Action Steps

There are numerous encrypted email solutions available to protect and ensure the confidentiality of your email. This will be determined by which option you choose to use: a web based email client, a desktop email client, or you may prefer a totally separate non-U.S. based encrypted email service.

There are several open-source PGP based encryption browser plug-ins available for Gmail. For example **Secure Gmail** extension for Chrome (https://www.streak.com/securegmail) is available from the Chrome web store.

- **Mailvelope** (https://www.mailvelope.com) is another free OpenPGP encryption browser extension for webmail. It can be used to secure email accounts not only in Gmail but also Yahoo, Outlook, and GMX all by default. Plus Mailvelope can be integrated into other web based email platforms. Mailvelope works as a plug-in for Google Chrome and Mozilla Firefox browsers.

In order to use Mailvelope, Secure Gmail, or any other PGP based solution to send encrypted messages, you need to ensure the party you want to exchange messages with also has a PGP email solution. Then you need to get and import their PGP public key. Anyone intercepting or opening an encrypted message in your mailbox will see random strings of numbers and letters that make no sense without the corresponding key pair to decrypt the message.

Note: while Mailvelope is free and open-source software, I always encourage everyone to give a donation for these free products. This helps support the continued development of privacy products like Mailvelope. Without user support, products like this cannot succeed long term.

- **GnuPG** (https://www.gnupg.org) is a free implementation of OpenPGP encryption for email. Here is a link with instructions on how to deploy GnuPG: https://emailselfdefense.fsf.org/en/

- **The Enigmail project** (https://www.enigmail.net) is a security extension to Mozilla Thunderbird. It works with GnuPG. Here is a quick start guide:

https://www.enigmail.net/documentation/quickstart.php

- **GPG for Mail** (https://gpgtools.org) is an open-source encryption plug-in for Apple Mail that runs on Mac OS X. The mail plug-in is part of the larger GPG Suite and supports from OS X 10.6 to 10.10 (Yosemite). This is the email encryption solution for Apple Mail users.

Encrypted Secure Email Solutions
As an alternative and probably easier for most people to use than the PGP based browser extensions mentioned above, there are several non-U.S. based privacy focused online email providers. Being based outside of the USA generally means not being subject to US legal restrictions and safe from at least some NSA snooping. Most of these companies charge for their private email services. These include companies such as:

Hushmail (www.hushmail.com) is a Canadian email provider with an easy to use encrypted email service.

Kolab Now email (https://kolabnow.com) is based in Switzerland where all data is securely stored and protected with stronger privacy legislation than is available in the USA or the EU. Plus they accept payment with Bitcoin giving some degree of anonymity.

ProtonMail (https://protonmail.ch) another Swiss based encrypted email provider with strong privacy protection.

Posteo (posteo.de) based in Germany offers a complete encrypted and private email solution.

MailPile (https://www.mailpile.is) is still in development. They are located in Iceland, another jurisdiction with strong privacy protection. MailPile will be a freeware PGP encryption mail solution that aims to be easier to use than current browser plug-in solutions.

Finally there is **Darkmail** (http://darkmail.info), which is still in development and looks to be the ultimate secure and private email solution. The teams behind both Lavabit (which was used by Edward Snowden) and Silent Circle are building Darkmail from the ground up to be the most secure email system available. More than a product, they are attempting to create an alliance of email providers to run Darkmail. They have stated that their goal is to get Microsoft, Yahoo, and Gmail to offer a Darkmail service. It looks very interesting.

Secure Instant Messaging: Action Steps

If you want to sent secure instant messages from your desktop rather than use AIM, MSN, Google Talk or Yahoo Messenger consider the following secure alternatives:

(For mobile phone encrypted messaging solutions see Chapter 10)

Adium (https://adium.im) is a free instant messaging application for Mac OSX that allows encrypted messaging. It can connect to numerous messaging products including Google Talk, MSN Messenger, Yahoo, AOL Instant messenger, ICQ, Twitter, and more. Adium uses OTR – off-the-record - encryption (https://otr.cypherpunks.ca)

Bitmessage (https://bitmessage.org) is an open-source P2P communications protocol to send encrypted messages. Available for Windows, Max OSX and Linux systems.

Webcams

Nearly all notebooks, tablets, game consoles, and smartphones have webcams as a standard feature. How many people, while in a meeting, have accidently switched theirs on and shared more than they wanted to? Or worse had someone with supervisor rights to their device spy on them via the webcam? The easy solution is to cover all web cams on all devices when not in use.

Webcams: Take Action Steps

- Install a removable lens cover when not using your webcam. This applies to webcams on PCs, laptops, tablets, or mobile phones.
  - ○ Inexpensive packs of removable, reusable webcam covers can be purchased from Amazon or similar stores. They are available in a variety of different sizes and can be re-used numerous times before losing adhesion.

WiFi

Home/Business WiFi

For most people, a home or business wireless network (WiFi) is the standard way to connect our computers, tablets, smartphones, and other connected devices to the web.

Without encryption enabled, your data can be captured and read by anyone who can connect to your WiFi. Most of the routers sold since 2006-2007 support WPA2 encryption. This is the strongest option to enable. Set a strong, unique password for your WiFi encryption.

Most WiFi routers come with a default password that also requires changing to stop unauthorized access to the router.

Public WiFi

Public WiFi is available everywhere today from coffee shops, churches, airports, shopping malls, and more. Anytime you see a WiFi spot offering "free WiFi" or "public WiFi" beware as data is easily intercepted.

Tools for WiFi monitoring and eavesdropping are freely available and can be used without too much technical skill. They are a real threat and make open, unsecure public WiFi networks dangerous to your privacy and the security of your data.

Most public WiFi networks are not secure. In March 2015, security firm Avast conducted research in major cities across the USA, Europe, and Asia to see how secure public WiFi really was.[81] Their results and findings lined up what cyber security professionals were saying. It confirmed that most public WiFi is not secure and users are unaware as to how open their communications actually are. In Chicago, 96% of all users connected to and used unsecure public networks. In New York, it was 91% and in San Francisco, 80%—all using and connecting to unsecure public networks. In addition to connecting to unsecure open WiFi networks, the researchers were able to see approximately half of all data traffic submitted by the users in the U.S. cities. If these researchers could access this information, so could any malicious hackers. Basically the online activities for at least 50% of the people using these networks would be in plain view for a hacker. The hacker would have had access to the following activities: read all emails; view all passwords; access to user names; watched users login to bank accounts; make online purchases; view photos; view videos; and look at the online browsing.

So there are still millions of people who perform online daily tasks over open, public WiFi networks. Their activities include logging on to online bank accounts, accessing email, updating social media, making online purchases, etc. The next time you go to a public WiFi hotspot (any coffee shop, airport, hotel, library, department store, etc.), stop and observe. You will see dozens of people using tablets, laptops, and smartphones. Most are totally oblivious to the fact that they are sending their data, unless encrypted, in plain text making it available to any hacker who decides to collect it.

Here is another crazy example of what goes on. In April 2015, a research report conducted by an anti-identity theft provider showed almost half of all Americans file their taxes online. Of those that file online, 65% use an open access WiFi network!

For many people it is simply a habit and they are unaware of the problems and risks associated with their online activities. This is how it often plays out: You have your phone or tablet with you while you drop in at your local coffee shop. You're automatically connected to their WiFi. However, you "forget" it's an unsecure network. You open your email or check your bank account online. You are not thinking about the risk. The world around you has changed but you are just enjoying your coffee and catching up online.

Rogue WiFi Hotspots

In addition to unsecure public WiFi, cyber criminals will deliberately set up rogue WiFi hotspots. These are often disguised in order to fool users into connecting. Criminals will use the same or similar names as popular venues, hoping to get visitors to automatically connect. So always check the name of the public WiFi hotspot before you connect. If it looks strange, give it a miss.

A safer option is to connect to the Internet using the cellular network rather than via public WiFi.

The dangers of using an unsecure WiFi hotspot can include:

- Snooping. Unless the data is encrypted, every site you visit and whatever you view over an open WiFi connection can be viewed by others.

- Whatever you send (including passwords, usernames, account numbers, etc.) can be copied.

- Software including spyware can be loaded onto your device.

Home/Business WiFi Gateway

Depending on your wireless gateway, you might have slightly different security setting options. If they are not clearly explained in the user manual, contact the manufacturer or your broadband provider for instructions on how to access your home routers settings.

Change the default security settings as follows:

- Change the default admin username and passwords to stop anyone from accessing and changing user settings. Most devices have the really unhelpful standard settings such as: user name = admin, password = password. Make sure you pick a strong password.

- Change the name of your network from the default. Some users get creative and use names like "FBI surveillance team" in order to scare hackers away. But don't use your real name or address to name your network.

- Hide your SSID. This is the name of your WiFi. If your SSID is not broadcasting, most casual rogue users won't know your WiFi even exists. Of course, this won't hide your WiFi from a pro.

- If encryption is not activated, you need to activate it. If you have a choice of encryption protocols to choose from, WPA2 is the most secure, next is WPA and least secure is WEP.

- If you know how to upgrade your router's firmware, do so to fix any known vulnerabilities.

- Disable remote management via the Internet.

- If you have added a WiFi extender, make sure it's also encrypted with WPA2. While WiFi extenders are useful to add extra range to your WiFi network, unless encryption is added, you have basically opened up a hole into your network that anyone can connect to.

Public WiFi
- Carefully check the name of any public WiFi network before you connect to it. If in doubt, double-check with the network owner to ensure you only connect to the correct network.

- Don't automatically accept connections to public WiFi hotspots. If possible, access the Internet via your cellular network.

- Use a VPN whenever you connect to a public WiFi network. (If you find you can't connect to the WiFi with a VPN it's either because the owner of the WiFi has only allowed HTTP and HTTPS protocols and blocked everything else, or there is a password on the WiFi.)

- As an additional safety measure, if you are not using a wireless network in an area with public WiFi, turn off/disable wireless networking on your system.

Note about VPN and TOR

Both VPNs and TOR are technologies used to preserve your anonymity online. While I'm totally fine with helping you remain anonymous online, it's not the intent of this book to provide information to help anyone commit criminal acts. So please don't do anything dumb while using TOR or a VPN.

VPN

A Virtual Private Network (VPN) is one of the most useful technologies to help preserve both security and privacy online.

A VPN provides an encrypted pipe through which your data traffic can flow from your device to a server owned by the VPN provider. The data then flows from the VPN's server to your destination website. This stops any service including your ISP from being able to read your data. All they would see if they looked is scrambled data. Secondly, once your data flows from the VPN servers to any website, the website has no way of knowing who you are or where you are as it only sees the traffic as having arrived from the VPN server. The only company in this scenario who can see your data is the VPN provider. So choosing a VPN provider you trust and who doesn't keep detailed traffic logs is paramount your privacy.

The benefits of using a VPN are:

• Ability to hide your true geographical location while online

• Prevent websites from tracking you

• The safest way to protect your data when connecting to a public WiFi

• Stop your ISP from being able to read your traffic

For the paranoid, paying your VPN provider with Bitcoin or some other crypto-currency provides them with far less personal details about who you actually are. Some VPN providers will also accept money order payments, which can be anonymous.

VPN: Take Action Steps

- Buy and install a VPN on all devices—smartphones, tablets and computers—that you use to connect to the Internet.
    - Many companies have a single license that covers numerous devices. So you don't need to purchase separate licenses for smartphones and computers.

- **F-Secure Freedome (https://www.f-secure.com/en/web/home_global/freedome)** is the VPN product I recommend. It is available for Windows, Mac, iPhone and Android devices. F-Secure has been around in the IT security market for many years building quality products. Freedome has an easy interface and hides much of the complexity of other VPN products.

    Their stance on VPN privacy is simple. *"We stand behind our commitment to privacy, and will never link the use of our products to your personal information!"* F-Secure is located in Finland and they are not required to follow EU data retention laws. So they do not collect any log files of websites visited when using their VPN service.

    In addition to providing anonymous web browsing, Freedome offers protection from malicious websites and web trackers.

    As for me, I already had several anti-tracking products installed on my laptop before I used

Freedome. So I was surprised to see Freedome finding additional web trackers. I checked with F-Secure about this. They told me that they use the same backend technology that is found in the anti-malware products to block malicious web pages and trackers. Another reason to like this product.

- **Hide My Ass** (https://www.hidemyass.com) is another excellent full featured VPN solution. The only potential downside for some people is HMA are located in the United Kingdom so are subject to EU privacy laws. If that concerns you then try F-Secure Freedome VPN

TOR

TOR is an acronym for The Onion Router. An anonymity network developed originally by the U.S. Navy as a way to communicate across the public Internet anonymously.

TOR is widely used by journalists, dissidents in foreign countries, activists, and others who want to hide their identity online. Many civil rights groups actively promote TOR to their followers. To its users and promoters, TOR is a way to throw off government surveillance. At the same time, TOR is used by criminals and those accessing the dark side of the Internet, the so-called Dark Web.

TOR as a product can be freely downloaded and used on Windows, Mac OSX, Linux/Unix, and Android. Once installed, TOR can be used as an alternative to a VPN as a way to secure communications. (See advantages and disadvantages of TOR vs. VPN below.)

The way TOR works is the key to making it so hard to track. Rather than sending data packets directly across the Internet from your client to the host web server you want to access, TOR passes encrypted packets around a random route bouncing traffic all over the place.

Volunteers run TOR relays or nodes, which are servers that pass TOR packets along its route. Each node only knows the node where the packet came from and the next node where the packet is going. None of the nodes know the entire route. And to top it all, the route that the data flows along changes all the time. It is just about impossible to track the data and know where it originated or where it's going.

While some TOR exit nodes could be monitored, the majority are not. And there is no way to determine who sent the traffic or where it originated. Therefore, the anonymity of the user is protected.

A word of caution: If you want to be totally secure even using TOR, encrypt any documents you send over the TOR network. A security researcher recently (June 2015) found some TOR exit nodes sniffing data to steal unencrypted passwords and sensitive information.

TOR vs. VPN Advantages and Disadvantages

Using either TOR or a VPN online are both ways to remain anonymous and bypass restrictive firewalls. While each technology works in a different way, they both basically keep the user's data anonymous. There are clear advantages to using each technology.

Advantages of using TOR include:
- Zero ability for anyone to track websites visited online.
- Free open-source software.
- No need to trust an ISP or VPN provider with your personal data when purchasing the "service."
- Considered the most secure option for anyone actively trying to hide their location.

Advantages of using a VPN include:

- High-speed web access versus TOR, which is generally slow. A VPN is a better choice if you intend to upload or download content.
- With a VPN service you know who runs the "anonymous" servers. TOR exit nodes can be set up and run by anyone.
- Simple to select any country servers you want your traffic to appear to be from. As long as the VPN service has its own servers in that location, any websites you visit see your traffic as from that particular country. Useful to access geo-restricted services.

For Advanced Users Only:

It is possible to run TOR over a VPN service. Doing so can add extra layers of privacy protection to your data. Details are beyond the scope of this book but freely available online. Alternatively check out JanusV (http://www.janusvm.com).

TOR: Take Action Steps

To download TOR:

- https://www.torproject.org/download/download. html.en
- Read the manual before using TOR.
- While the software is free, it's good to donate!

Summary

If you have followed all the Action StepsTake Acton steps in this chapter, congratulations! You should have a lot more peace of mind in knowing that you are now more secure and have more online privacy than the majority of the population. If not, take a highlighter pen, a post-it note, or whatever works for you and mark all the steps where you still need to take action.

Chapter 9

Secure Yourself Online

*This chapter deals with securing yourself online using traditional laptop and computer devices. The chapter following this one looks at securing yourself online when using mobile devices—smartphones and tablets.

"Anything that is happening on the web today is pretty much completely unregulated. There's really no oversight and there's no real standards either."
Tim Libert, University Pennsylvania researcher

Search Engines

Every time you use an Internet search engine, be it Google, Yahoo Search, or Bing, the search query terms and other data are recorded. Over time the large search engine companies have built up huge databases of everything you have ever searched for online. It doesn't matter if you delete your browsing history, that's only a local record in your browser. Google, Bing, and Yahoo have a copy of your search data on their servers.

The data they collect includes:
- The actual search query terms as typed into the search bar
- Your IP address
- ID tracking cookies
- The time and date of the search
- Any links clicked on when the results were returned to you

If you have a Google account and are logged in when you use Google Search, even more personal data is collected. This includes your name, email, and other personal identifying information. The same applies to using Yahoo Search. This very precise information has enabled the search engine giants to build the most detailed datasets on individual interests ever collected.

Naturally this data is a goldmine for advertisers, marketers, and governments. They are all very interested in what you are searching for and looking at online.

According to a 2012 research poll conducted by the Pew Research Group, the majority of American Internet users are satisfied by the quality of the search results they get back from search engines. At the same time however, most are concerned about the collection of their personal data and by targeted advertising.[82]

Google

Google's search engine receives around 3.5 billion search inquires a day. That equates to approximately 88% of the worldwide search engine market. Having such a dominant market share means Google knows more about what the world is searching for than any other technology vendor. This has given Google a huge competitive advantage and has allowed them to expand into numerous other markets.

By cleverly monetizing the enormous amounts of data they collect about Internet user's likes, habits, and interests, Google has made a fortune for its shareholders.

The downside of Google's search technology is obvious. They have linked searches to individual IP addresses and with data mining, have collected masses of information on individual users. It is fair to reason that Google knows more about our intimate details and us than our best friends do!

Google keeps all the data it collects indefinitely.[83] However in the USA, they anonymize the server data logs after 18 to 24 months. They only share aggregated anonymized data with their partners and advertisers. As mentioned elsewhere in this book, there have been numerous research reports debunking the data anonymization myth. [84] Computer scientists have shown the flaw in the thinking behind what is and what is not personal information. They contend that all data is personal when combined with enough other relevant data bits. [85] *(See "the anonymity problem" in Chapter 5 for more info.)*

Other Search Engines

Just like Google, Yahoo Search and Bing collect a huge amount of personally identifiable information whenever you search using their online search engines.

It seems that Yahoo Search retains data for 18 months, thereafter they de-anonymize it. Bing deletes users' IP address data after six months, a big improvement from their previous 18-month retention period. So while Bing doesn't retain search data for as long as Yahoo or anywhere near as long as Google, they still keep records on your searches.

Search Engines: Take Action Steps

To enable private web searching without being tracked by the search engine, use one of the privacy-minded options listed below for all online searching:

- **DuckDuckGo** (www.duckduckgo.com)
- **Disconnect Search** (disconnect.me/search)
- **Ixquick** (ixquick.com)

Website Privacy and Security

All websites collect information from their online visitors. Some go much further than others in tracking you and then selling the information to marketers.

For instance, most people would expect a site like WebMD (the popular online medical website) to keep confidential the particular medical condition users are searching for and viewing on their website. Not so! WebMD captures that information, including the medical conditions being researched, plus your computer IP address and then sells that information to private marketing companies and data brokers. So while having the same private discussion with a doctor, it would remain private and protected under HIPPA regulations. Looking at medical information online has a distinct lack of privacy. The same happens when you use the CDC (Center for Disease Control) website. Any search data is sent to Google. [86]

This tracking and selling of search information happens on the majority of online information sites. Either via hidden online trackers (see section on Website Trackers), or by collecting any information you type into search boxes on the website or online forum.

Web Browser Security and Privacy: Take Action Steps

All browsers have numerous settings to increase your online privacy and security. Additionally, there is a growing number of third party browser plug-ins and extensions you can apply. Several are detailed below.

Another good option to increase online anonymity is to always use a VPN *(see section on VPNs for more details).*

Browser Settings*

Browser settings change often, as new features are added and new versions released. Although settings may be different from those mentioned, the features described would still be in most browsers although you might need to look for them. Some may be enabled by default, others will be located under advanced features.

Privacy and security settings to enable:

- **Automatic updates.** Some browsers like Firefox are set to automatically update by default. In Chrome if you don't get an automatic update, select the "About Google Chrome." Chrome will automatically check for any updates. Click "Relaunch" to apply any updates found.
    - If you have the option in your browser, select to be warned if the upgrade will disable any of your add-ons.

- **Search engine**. Set your default search engine to DuckDuckGo. *(See section on search engines for more details.)*

- Block **Pop-up windows**. Another function that will be taken care of by using the suggested add-ons. But likewise if your add-on gets disabled, enable pop-up blocking in all browsers. You might come across a website that needs to use a pop-up window, like a banking website. If so, enable the pop-ups just for that website.

- **Do Not Track (DNT)** feature. This is available in most browsers and should be enabled. While there is no requirement that websites comply with DNT, many do.

- Enable a warning when sites try to **install add-ons.** You should be in charge of any add-ons. Websites that try to install software on your system without your permission are normally up to no good.

- In most browsers, **Internet plug-ins** such as Adobe Flash, Silverlight, and Java run by default. As mentioned elsewhere in this book, hackers often attack systems by exploiting unpatched vulnerabilities in these plug-ins. Use your browser setting to restrict when plug-ins play. Look under "manage website settings" in your browser.

(See section on updating applications for information on keeping browser plug-ins updated.)

- **Microphone and camera settings**. Make sites ask if they require access to your microphone and camera settings. If there is no good reason, simply deny them access.

- **Location settings.** Don't allow websites access to your location services, again unless there is a good reason.

Website Trackers

Cookies

Cookies are small data files placed on your computer by a website you visit in order for the website to recognize and remember information about you, like an ID card. Regular cookies or 1st party cookies are not malware of any sort and are required on many websites. Typically, cookies are set to track user preferences like language settings and user authentication. With cookies, you won't have to re-enter information when you re-visit a site. Lastly, cookies collect and compile anonymous, aggregated data that is used for analytics. Only the website that serves the cookie to your browser is able to read the information in the cookie.

Tracking Cookies

The primary way online advertisers and marketers track users and deliver customized content is through the placement of tracking cookies on popular websites. These are also referred to as third party or third domain tracking cookies. They are placed on the website by a third party and share information with numerous other sites.

174

When you visit a website, the content on the site typically belongs to that site. However, ads that are displayed are delivered to the website from a third party ad server that specializes in ad placement.

Many popular websites contain numerous cross-domain tracking cookies for the purpose of tracking and delivering customized ads. For instance, on the *Wall Street Journal's* homepage, Disconnect (a privacy program that reveals tracking cookies among other things), counted 54 individual third party tracking cookies. That's 54 individual advertising and marketing networks that have placed tracking cookies on this website in order to identify web visitors, where they came from, and what they are looking at.

To put that into context, imagine if 54 advertisers followed you around the mall and into individual shops, looking over your shoulder to see what you are doing and interested in. That would freak you out! Yet online marketing companies act as if you don't care. They must think that if you can't see what they are doing (since tracking cookies are hidden unless you know where to find them), their behavior doesn't matter. Bear in mind that what they are doing is totally legal. They want to better understand and profile you as an individual in order to send you "targeted ads." However, most of us are not fine with this behavior.

An interesting note on tracking cookies is that it's not just advertising networks that use them to identify individuals. There are numerous articles detailing how both the NSA and Britain's GCHQ were able to manipulate and use Google tracking cookies to track individuals across websites.[87]

Web Beacons

Web beacons are invisible objects embedded on a web page for the purpose of measuring and analyzing usage and activity.

They are also referred to as web bugs, pixel trackers, or clear GIFs. They are placed by third party ad servers and used in conjunction with cookies to record visitor behavior on websites.

You can't opt out of web beacons because they are embedded in the pages of websites. However, by blocking all tracking cookies, you will disable any web beacons from tracking your activity on a website and linking it to a specific device.

Website Trackers: Take Action Steps

All modern web browsers allow users to disable cookies. Some such as Safari block all third party tracking cookies by default.

- Disable third party/advertising cookies in browser settings or preferences. While the add-ons in the section below do the same thing, in case they get disabled, always block third party tracking cookies in all browsers. Most third party tracking cookies serve customized ads that you really don't need and they slow your system down. Get rid of them.

In addition to blocking tracking cookies in your browser settings, it's important to use one of the following products to block third party tracking cookies and web beacons. Some ultra sneaky advertising companies deliberately bypass third party cookie blocking. The browser extensions below will stop them. You don't need them all (that would be redundant), so choose the one you like and add to all your browsers on all devices that you use online.

- **Ghostery** (http://www.ghostery.com) is a freeware, cross platform privacy browser extension. Add Ghostery to all web browsers on all devices, enable tracker library auto-updates, and select "all" in the tracker section. **(Important note: No trackers are selected by default, so make**

sure you select them all during set-up or else Ghostery won't block them.)

- **Disconnect** (https://disconnect.me) is available for Windows, Mac, Android, and iOS. Apart from blocking tracking cookies, Disconnect has several additional privacy features. It's available in both free and upgraded paid for editions.

- **Privacy Badger**
  (https://www.eff.org/privacybadger) from the Electronic Freedom Foundation is another excellent solution to block website trackers and online ads. It is currently available for Chrome and Firefox. Note at the time of this writing that Privacy Badger was incompatible with Avast anti-virus, which for some reason blocked it. So if you use Avast, rather go with Ghostery or Disconnect.

- For more technical users, the **NoScript** Mozilla Firefox browser extension (https://noscript.net) is useful to control JavaScript, Java, Adobe Flash, and other plug-ins. It only allows them to run on trusted websites. NoScript does what it says. It blocks all scripts until you authorize them. Some may find it less convenient as it increases security. (NoScript is free so don't forget to donate when you download this useful software.)

Flash Cookies

Multimedia applications use Flash cookies. These cookies are turned on by default in Adobe Flash player to store information on computers that they might want to use later. Flash cookies are also referred to as locally shared objects (LSO's) or super-cookies.

In an attempt to override web visitors deleting regular cookies, Flash cookies have been used on some sites to stealthily re-spawn or re-create regular HTTP cookies that have been deleted. Anything can be stored as a Flash cookie including websites visited or whatever data is typed into a browser. Many websites that store Flash cookie information don't always mention it even in their privacy settings.

It's estimated that over 90% of all Internet connected computers use Adobe Flash to play video and other multimedia content, so this approach to tracking can be widespread. Currently there's no easy way to tell if Flash cookies are tracking you or not.

Because Flash cookies are stored by Adobe Flash Player and not in a browser, they can be used to track all the web activity originating from one computer, not just from one individual browser. (Cross browser tracking.)

Flash Cookies: Take Action Steps

Change the default settings for Adobe Flash to restrict Flash cookies at
http://www.macromedia.com/support/documentation/en/flashplayer/help/settings_manager03.html

- Under **Global Storage settings** tab, move the slider bar to zero and click **Never ask again**
- Uncheck both the other boxes (Allow third-party content and Store common components).

Install **CCleaner** (www.piriform/ccleaner) to clean out any saved Flash cookie information saved on your system.

- Select the **Applications** tab, check the box for **Abobe Flash Player**, to delete saved flash cookies.

Digital marketing companies are constantly looking for new ways to identify and track individual users both on specific sites and across the web. Due to the now widespread practice of deleting tracking cookies and using ad-blockers, several alternative harder to delete browser fingerprinting techniques are being tested and deployed. One of the sneakier techniques being used by some online advertising networks is canvas fingerprinting. This is used to track site visitors without the involvement of any cookies.[88]

Canvas fingerprinting works by taking advantage of the Canvas API that's found inside your web browser. The website hosting the canvas fingerprinting script paints an image on a hidden HTML canvas element. Then a snapshot is taken of it before posting the snapshot back to itself. Because the exact pixel values in the drawn image will differ subtly from one browser to the next, the website can use those differences to distinguish between each visitor as well as to recognize returning visitors. By sharing this information among websites in the advertising network and combining it with additional known visitor data from those websites, it's possible to identify a unique individual. Of course, all without the user's knowledge or consent.

It's difficult to find out exactly how widespread this sneaky practice is. Researchers from Princeton and KU Leven Universities have done most of the work uncovering canvas fingerprinting. They estimate around 5% of the top 100,000 webservers are using it. Since their original research was conducted in 2014, it could be more or less now. Additionally, many of the companies involved would like to keep this information hidden, making any estimates difficult.

Websites using this creepy tracking technology include many household names and surprisingly even a few IT security vendors. Looking through the 5,000 websites recorded in the

179

joint Princeton University/KU Leuven University research report, there wasn't any one particular category, apart from porn and news sites that stood out. The websites were spread all over the world and across most industries.

For example, some of the company sites named in the report included:

- Large brands: Starbucks, Hilton Hotels, Adidas, Allstate Insurance, Expedia.com, AOL, Groupon

- Telecom and technology providers: British Telecom, SAP, Canon, Huawei, Sony, SAS, Dropbox

- IT security vendors: Kaspersky, Comodo, CA Technologies, Ariva

- Government websites: Whitehouse.gov, USCIS.gov, DHS.gov, Social security.gov

- Many newspapers and news sites

- As to be expected, numerous porn sites

Please note the list above includes websites that were running canvas fingerprinting scripts on their homepages as of May 1-5, 2014.[89] Some websites may have already removed this form of tracking and others may have added it. This is only an illustration of the kind of organizations that were tracking visitors using canvas fingerprinting scripts at the time of the original research.

Social bookmarking company AddThis is the leading vendor supplying canvas fingerprinting to websites. They offer an opt out option on their website. This adds a cookie into your browser that they claim will stop their client websites from collecting a canvas fingerprint of your browser. However, as the KU Leuven and Princeton University researchers pointed out in their research, clicking the "AddThis" opt out button didn't seem to make any difference to how the tracking platform treated them and continued to collect their data! [90]

Just as with all tracking technology, many companies believe it is their inherent right to collect as much information from you and about you whenever they interact with you online. This is so ingrained into many marketing organizations that they don't really believe in user privacy. Deploying canvas fingerprinting as a replacement for tracking cookies that they know most users dislike and disable is a sign of their intent to carry on tracking you in any way they can.

Canvas Fingerprinting: Take Action Steps

Canvas fingerprinting operates via Javascript. So you might think the easy option would be to simply disable Javascript. But that would disable many regular sites, so it's not an option.

There are, however, several browser extensions that work.

- While **Ghostery** does block the AddThis network, (the main culprits spreading canvas fingerprinting), there is nothing to stop other ad networks from using the same technique. So make sure you have **Ghostery** added to all your browsers on all devices. Then enable tracker library auto-updates and select all in the tracker section (no trackers are selected by default, so ensure you select them all upon installation).

- **Canvas FingerprintBlock** is a Chrome browser extension that will protect your privacy and prevent any webpages using canvas fingerprint scripts from tracking your browser. Once installed it will return a blank canvas to the script thus fooling it. You can find it in the Google Chrome web store.

- **CanvasBlocker** is a Mozilla Firefox browser extension that will prevent the Javascript canvas API from working. There are several different modes and settings you will have to pay attention to. Some websites may not work correctly, but at least you get to choose between whitelisting or blacklisting them.
    - An Android version of CanvasBlocker is currently under development.

- Using the **TOR web browser** is another option. In 2012, TOR added a feature to notify users when a website attempts to use the canvas feature. And it sends a blank canvas image back. However, TOR can be slow and it's not suitable for some applications (multimedia apps), but it will effectively block device and canvas fingerprinting.

Chapter 10

Security and Privacy for Mobile Devices

"App stores and mobile apps are the greatest hostile code and malware delivery mechanism ever created."

Winn Schwartau, chairman Mobile Active Defense

According to Pew Research Group, two-thirds of the population in the United States owns a smartphone and adoption rates continue to grow. Likewise, tablet computer sales are surging ahead according to every market report.

As the shift from desktop to mobile devices continues, our smartphones and tablets are containing more sensitive and personal information, and we are using them to access all sorts of online services. Our smartphones also "know" more about us than we realize. For instance, they know who our friends are from our contact lists. They know where we go from the GPS data. From the apps we use, plus our Internet browsing, they gather the details and know what interests us.

With the huge increase in smartphones and tablets has come an even bigger increase in mobile applications (apps). Technology research group Gartner believes 102 billion apps were downloaded in 2013. They forecast more than double that to 268 billion downloads in 2017.[91] If we add in the rise of wearable and connected IoT devices, all indications are that the growth in mobile devices and applications is set to soar for the foreseeable future.

It's not surprising that this massive growth in mobile devices, and the sort of information they contain, has drawn the attention of cyber criminals and malware developers. According to security firm Webroot, in 2013 they had collected around 250,000 malicious mobile apps, which were designed to steal data from smartphones. By mid-2014, this number had jumped to over a million and the list continues to grow.

So while the mobile application you have just downloaded may perform a useful function, at the same time it could be compromising your privacy and accessing the data on your phone.

Mobile Device Security and Privacy Best Practices: Take Action Steps

It's imperative to think of your smartphone and other mobile devices as mini computers. So you need to apply all the same rules to your phone and tablet as you do to any other computer or device that holds personal data. In fact, mobile devices often hold more personal data than your laptop. You not only have data files, but also photos, videos, and contact lists on your mobile devices.

Smartphone and Tablet Security Basics:
(I know this is a long list, but all are important if you want to protect your data and privacy.)

- Set a secure **PIN** as your first line of defense to protect all smartphones and mobile devices. Yes it's not as convenient to have to enter a PIN every time you want to access some feature, but if you ever lose your phone, you will be very glad you created a secure password. Additionally, set your password to be required after X amount of idle time. This will prevent anyone picking up your unattended phone and stealing your information.

- Apart from adding a secure PIN, if your device offers a **two-factor authentication** option, enable it. This will add additional logon security.
  - **Authy** (https://www.authy.com) is a useful option to add two-factor authentication to secure mobile applications.

- Avoid "**jailbreaking**" (iOS devices) or "**rooting**" (Android devices) on your phone. Jailbreaking and rooting is a process that allows access to the operating system in order to change privilege escalation, add additional applications, and extend the features of a device. Doing so makes most phones less secure and more open to being exploited.

- Near Field Communication (**NFC**) uses radio to communicate. NFC is found on many Android and Windows devices and was introduced by Apple on the iPhone 6 (to enable Apple Pay). Hackers have already developed attacks to steal device contents using NFC. Unless it's really needed for some application, it's easier to simply disable NFC. In addition, Android users should disable Android beam, which uses NFC to exchange data with other Android devices.

- Make regular **Backup** copies of any files, photos, videos, and other data that has value. *(See section on Backups.)*

- To add extra security to personal information, **Encrypt** your data files on your mobile device. If your phone is also used at work as part of a BYOD system to access business data, the business should provide encryption. *(See section on Encryption.)*

- Apply **operating system updates**. Not updating to the latest version of the operating system leaves your devices more vulnerable and open to attack. *(See section on Application Updates and Patching.)*

- If you access the Internet on your mobile devices, install a VPN on them. **F-Secure Freedome**, my recommendation for VPN protection, is an easy to use solution. It will protect you when using public WiFi. Freedome is available for Android, iOS, and the Kindle Fire OS.

- When it's time to replace your phone, make sure you have completely removed all your personal information, contacts, passwords, photos, and videos from your old device.
    o First backup all data to your computer.
    o On an iPhone or iPad, go to "Settings," "General," scroll down to "Reset" and then choose "Erase all Content and Settings." This will wipe the data.
    o On an Android device, the instructions may vary depending on the manufacturer. However there are two options to delete all your data. First you can do a factory reset. This will erase all data. If you want to be extra safe and ensure no data can be recovered, you can use a third party product like **Avast Anti-Theft** (https://www.avast.com/en-us/anti-theft), (it's a free download). Anti-theft has a remote secure delete feature. So once you have installed the app on your phone, log-into your online Avast account and remotely wipe the phone.

Smartphones are often referred to by privacy professionals as the spy or tracking device in your pocket for a good reason. It's an apt description. Many people never leave home without their mobile devices. So if you can track a phone you will know where the owner is.

If you read the privacy policy of mobile phone carriers, you will find references and descriptions of "precise" and "real-time location services" used to track you. Also listed will be something along the lines of unspecified "partners and licenses" who may collect and use your location data. That's a nice way of saying that they can and will collect data on where you go, they will use their services to track you, and will also allow their business partners to do the same.

These are various location-monitoring services built into our mobile devices that are used to locate and track us, usually without our knowledge. If you track this over a period of time, it produces a very detailed pattern of an individual's life and habits.

Your smartphone constantly leaks location data. This happens in many different ways.

GPS Tracking
All smartphones contain global positioning sensors that link the location of the phone to the satellite based global positioning network. This location data is used by applications such as local weather reporting and mapping apps to provide location services. You can opt out by disabling location services.

If you disable your location services on your mobile phone, you lose the functionality of some useful apps. If you need to use the maps feature, or check local weather, the more secure option would be to check an online map or weather service via a WiFi hotspot. With a VPN enabled, this will hide your true location, and in addition will secure your data.

If you can't access WiFi you can simply re-enable location services and switch off all other services apart from the ones you need. Once you are finished with the services, disable location services again and delete the location history off your phone.

Cell Tower Tracking

Smartphones can be tracked using cell tower triangulation or multilateration technology (MLAT) to pinpoint their exact location. The whereabouts of your cellphone as collected by the cellular network is part of the meta-data that's collected about you and your mobile device. While it's possible to turn-off the GPS location service on a smartphone, it's not possible to stop your phone from connecting to a cell tower unless you remove the battery or totally isolate the phone inside a secure RF signal blocking case that cuts all cellphone signals.

WiFi Tracking

Many venues such as retail locations, sports arenas, and airports use MLA (Mobile Location Analytics) to track individual mobile phones by capturing their WiFi, MAC, and Bluetooth addresses. (*For more information, see Mobile Location Analytics in Chapter 10.*)

RF (Radio Frequency) shielding bags are one way to completely stop WiFi, cellular, and Bluetooth signals from connecting to wireless devices. However, the majority of cheap, low-end RF blocking soft phone cases sold online are of dubious quality and don't fully cut off all signals. Law enforcement quality evidence bags, like the Black Hole Faraday bags, which are used for the seizure and shielding of electronic equipment, are a real solution.

Some cheap RF signal blocking bags may appear to work when tested inside a building that is located several miles from the nearest cellphone tower. However, it's often found that the blocking is not from the bag but from walls, obstacles, trees, and distance degrading the cell signal. A quick test to tell if the bag is fully blocking all cellular signals is to test the bag with the phone inside within 300 ft. or closer to an actual cellphone tower. Put the phone in the bag and seal it. Then from another phone try to call and send an SMS message to the phone in the bag. If anything gets through, the bag doesn't provide any real protection.

Location Services—Privacy Issues

The biggest concern with location data is the purpose for its use. Numerous companies and apps keep track of you when you have always-on location data. Among them are Apple (iPhones), Google (Android phones), FourSquare (app), RunKeeper (app), and Facebook messenger (app). Users of these services and apps have consented to being tracked 24/7. There are some options to limit or opt out. At least in the case of all these apps, you know why they want your data.

Things get a little greyer with companies like Uber who have already managed to get a bad record regarding data privacy. They collect a customer's location data even when they are not riding in an Uber car! Uber already knows the customer's email and credit card details, which are all the information required to provide their service. However, from July 2015, its app adds always-on location data collection. The company doesn't tell its customers why it requires the data, which would give the customer the choice of whether to allow it. At the time of writing, several privacy groups are calling for this type over-collecting of personal data to be banned.[92]

Another privacy concern tied to the collection of location data is the secondary use of the data collected. Many businesses that collect mobile phone location data share this information with their business partners. So you may consent to allow a primary company to collect your location data as it relates to their services you use. However, when they pass it on to unnamed business partners, what happens to your location data then? What is it being used for? The purpose of location data is only to show where you are and where you have been. In other words, it's perfect for tracking. It's important to know who has it and why they need it. What if one of the "business partners" who has your location tracking information passed on to them is your insurance company? They would identity you from your email, address, or phone number. By purchasing your location data, they can tell where you spend your time. If they notice you go by fast food restaurants or frequent a lot of bars, they could adjust your premiums based solely on this information.

Also what happens when the business partner who now has your exact location data goes out of business? Who gets your data and what will it be used for? Any former privacy policy is essentially history. The data can be used for any purpose, including being added into a larger profile of your life. If a data broker purchases it, it will be added to your profile. Maybe the location data will be used in the background check for your next job.

All of a sudden you might decide it's not such a good idea to allow yourself to be tracked everywhere.

Location Services: Take Action Steps

GPS Tracking

- **Apple iOS,** to turn off location services go to "Settings," "Privacy," and disable "Location services."

- **Android,** open "Settings," scroll to "Location," "Google Location Services," and choose "Off." Then tap "Location history," choose "Off." Lastly tap "Delete location history."

- **Windows Phone,** access "Settings," choose "Location," and "Off."

Cellphone tower tracking. If you want to completely make your phone disappear off the cellular, WiFi, and GPS networks, use a **Black Hole Faraday bag**.

WiFi tracking: Disable WiFi and Bluetooth before venturing out. This will stop your mobile device from trying to connect to WiFi networks that could be used to collect the MAC address on your device.

Photo GPS and Geolocation Data

Every time you take a photo with a digital camera or phone, a file is created, saved, and stored on your device. This is typically a JPEG image.

Along with the actual bits of the image, there is a huge amount of additional data about the photo that is recorded. This is metadata (which is data about image). It includes the standard information such as the time and date the photo was taken and the camera settings used. If the device has GPS capabilities, as all smartphones do, then geolocation metadata is recorded as well. This will pinpoint the location where the photo was taken which is used to view locations on a map and to geo-tag data. So for instance, you could view other photos taken in the same location.

The problem for those who don't want to be tracked is that geolocation metadata can be extracted from images. It can be used to determine the location where the photo was taken. Therefore, the "where and when" of people in a photo can be revealed.

Some journalists, law enforcement and investigators are skilled in knowing how this trick works and have used geolocation metadata from images to trace the location of individuals in photos.

The Associated Press (AP) used geolocation data taken from Instagram account images of Congressman Rep. Aaron Schock to help determine when he had used private flights.[93] The AP crosschecked this against flight data for an article on the congressman's expenses.

Journalists also used metadata from images posted to social media accounts of Russian soldiers in Syria to reveal their true locations. This proving they were operating outside of areas that the Kremlin had reported they were active in.

Likewise in 2014, data security pioneer John McAfee, while on the run in Central America, was tracked down and arrested in Guatemala. He had been laying low trying to avoid capture in connection with an ongoing investigation into the murder of his neighbor in Belize. A reporter who was accompanying him used his iPhone 4S to take a photo and upload it to the Internet without first stripping the all-revealing geolocation metadata out. This gave away the exact location of the residence where McAfee was hiding. [94]

Photo GPS and Geolocation Data: Take Action Steps

If you want to share images with friends online and want to remove the photo GPS and geolocation data, there are several options.

Most current smartphone operating systems have the option to disable GPS and geographic tagging data in their settings.

- **Apple iOS**, access "Settings," "Privacy," then under "Location services," toggle "Camera" off

If you have images that still have geo-tag information you can remove that as well. There are numerous third party apps that will strip out the EXIF data, which includes GPS and location details of where the photo was taken.

Photo Investigator is one such app, available from iTunes. It will remove photo metadata from images on iPhones and iPads. There are similar apps available for Android and other platforms.

Mobile Internet Access

Mobile devices—smartphones and tablets—contain treasure troves of personal information for hackers to steal and big businesses to gather. For the more traditional PC and laptop user, they are not as likely to have installed security or privacy enhancing protection of their data. This is unfortunate as most mobile devices are a huge security and privacy risk. They contain lists of contacts, personal photos, emails, financial data, and in many cases corporate and business information. According to Pew Research Center, more than half of U.S. smartphone users do banking online[95] and 78% use their phone to make online purchases. This alone makes mobile devices a very attractive target for cyber criminals.

Of the three largest mobile operating systems, Android is without a doubt the most unsecure. There are numerous security research reports that reveal the huge (and ever growing) number of malicious Android apps and malware. Adding to the problem, according to security group Sophos, as recently as February 2015, over 40% of Android users were using old versions of Android. That leaves their devices open to old operating system bugs and exploits.

Cross Device Tracking

Marketing firms try numerous methods to track us on the mobile web. Being able to track online users across multiple devices is the Holy Grail for marketing and technology companies. Unlike the days when a PC-based browser could be tracked by data cookies and tied to a user, tracking consumers who use multiple devices, including smartphones to access online digital services, is not as easy.

There are two broad categories that cross device-tracking falls into. These are "deterministic" (which uses authenticated logins) and "probabilistic" (the use of statistics to determine probability).

Of the two, "deterministic" tracking is the easiest for technology vendors and those with a direct client relationship to deploy. By forcing users to login to their service for every device they use, companies like Facebook, Twitter, and Google are all able to link multiple devices back to an individual user.

To block tracking cookies is fairly simple. But limiting mobile app vendors and marketers from tracking you across all your devices (laptop, tablet, smartphone, wearable devices, etc.) is not so simple. For example, if you don't want Facebook to track you on your tablet, smartphone, or Internet connected smart TV, don't sign into Facebook on those devices. If you do, Facebook will link the digital fingerprint of your device to your authenticated account.

Mobile Internet: Take Action Steps

Secure Browsing:
Mobile TOR browsing is available for both Android and iOS phones. (See section on TOR for more details.) There are numerous TOR apps available. These are good options:

- Android: For the extra cautious, you can replace your standard web browser with secure alternative, **Orbot** (https://guardianproject.info/apps/orbot) from the Guardian Project. Orbot is a free proxy app to access the TOR network. It's a solid solution to encrypt mobile web traffic and to defend against surveillance. TOR is slower than using a VPN but if used correctly, it's the safest method for anonymous web access.

- iOS: Use the **Onion Browser** that is configured to connect to the TOR network. Available on iTunes and the Apple App store.

Secure Voice Apps:

There are are a growing number of secure encrypted voice apps available to choose from.

- **Silent Circle** (silentcircle.com) is a secure calling app for both iOS and Android for those concerned about the security and privacy of their communications. Silent Circle encrypts calls, texts, video calls, and file transfers.

- **Silent Circle** (silentcircle.com) is also the maker of the secure encrypted smartphone, **Blackphone** that runs on its own priority operating system. Built from the ground up as a secure device, it's probably the most secure phone available to private individuals. A good option for executives, politicians, or anyone else who really wants to keep their secrets secure.

- Another option for secure encrypted calls and texting is to use the free open-source **Signal app (formally separate apps, Red Phone and Textsecure)** from Open Whisper Systems (https://whispersystems.org). Both parties use the same service to send encrypted texts or make encrypted calls. Signal works by encrypting your voice and/or text messages and routing them through your network data and not over the cellular network. It's a smart solution and will stop mobile couriers (and anyone else) from capturing the encrypted data—and it's free. (Don't forget to donate if you download the software).

Secure Messaging Apps:

While the three largest messaging apps are easy to use, (WhatsApp - with 30 billion messages sent a day, Facebook Messenger and Snapchat), there are more secure alternatives.

- **CryptoCat** (https://crypto.cat) is another open-source secure chat and file transfer solution that integrates with the browser on your smartphone. CryptoCat also integrates with Facebook messenger, allowing you to see if any of your FB contacts are also using it.

- Wickr (https://www.wickr.com) is a solid encrypted messaging service that encrypts both messages and key delivery. It's available for both iOs and Android devices. With strong admin controls, Wickr is a good choice for organizations to deploy.

Mobile Applications

"Trustworthy apps fell from 52% in 2013 to 28% in 2014."
"We are discovering a large quantity of malicious apps every day at an alarming growing rate."
Webroot 2015 Threat Brief

The many thousands of available mobile apps that add functionality to smartphones are often the very openings that are leaking personal information and other data from mobile devices. From private information exfiltration (stealing private data off your device), to key logging and screen scraping (stealing information off your screen as you enter it), to installing backdoors (allowing hackers access to your device), malicious apps do all of this and more.

Cyber criminals, malware writers, and malicious app coders are all focusing more on the mobile market due to its high growth and the low levels of security products installed on mobile devices. In addition, growing numbers of users access their banking and other financial sites via their unprotected mobile devices. To cyber criminals this is a unique opportunity to infect, take over, and steal money from mobile device owners.

According to mobile security firm Webroot, in 2013 they collected around 250,000 malicious apps. By mid-2014, this number had jumped to over a million malicious apps.

Webroot's findings on suspicious and malicious mobile apps are in line with those from other security researchers at almost every other security firm, all of who concur that malicious mobile apps are a growing risk for mobile device users.

The majority of problem apps run on the Android mobile operating system.[96] The reason for this is the different ways that Apple and Google have approached the market. Apple locks down what can be loaded onto their devices with all third party iOS apps only available through the Apple App store. When developers submit apps to the Apple Store it takes on average 3-4 weeks for Apple to thoroughly check and approve them. This helps eliminate most rogue or malware apps. On the other hand, Google has an open-eco-system approach. This allows malware writers to submit their malicious code hidden inside legitimate looking apps to numerous third party Android app stores with the hope of infecting more users. The strategy works, and many free Android apps that are not on the official Google Play app store have been found to contain malicious code.

Google Play

The official Google Play app store is the largest resource for Android apps and this makes it a big target for malware writers. Even while Google is constantly tightening up the checking of apps prior to allowing them onto Google Play, many that act in a malicious fashion are fake, or contain malware that still slips through the cracks. Google uses a malware filter to catch malicious apps before developers upload them, at least that's what is supposed to happen.

Malicious Apps on Google Play

Some recent examples illustrated below show the type of malicious apps Android malware writers manage to sneak into Google Play:

- Cowboy Adventure was a game that contained a trojan designed to steal Facebook credentials. It was downloaded approximately a million times. Upon launching the app, users were greeted with a fake Facebook login screen. If they filled in their details, these were sent to the app developer in Eastern Europe who was able to then access the users' Facebook accounts.

- A second game named Jump Chess from the same company, Tinker Studio, used the same fake login popup screen in order to steal Facebook user names and passwords.

In both of these cases, the malware developers used a crafty hack to bypass the Google Play checks. The trojan hidden in the games only activated itself when it sensed a non-U.S. or Canadian IP address. Thereby, it was missed by Google's Play Store Bouncer malware filter as the hidden trojan was dormant. Both games have since been removed from the Play Store.[97]

- Popular mobile app Dubsmash is another example. It caught the attention of researchers at Avast in April 2015 who checked it out. It seems malware developers had been slipping fake Dubsmash apps that contained links to porn sites into the Play Store. Following up the original find, security firm

ESet discovered a further 51 fake apps loaded on the Play Store, all containing the so-called "Android Clicker Trojan." The fake apps were downloaded at least 300,000 before being discovered and removed by Google. These included fake copies of games: Batman 2, The Walking Dead 2, Rally Racer 2, Deer Hunter 2015, Minecraft 3, and a host of others.[98]

Fake Security Apps

As if downloading an app only to find it contains malware isn't annoying enough, how about paying for and downloading a security app, only to find out it's fake and does nothing? A few years ago, the scam of selling do-nothing fake computer anti-virus software was popular online. Malicious developers have repeated the same scam with mobile anti-malware products this time.

In early 2014, security firm Kaspersky found a copy of their anti-malware product, Kaspersky Mobile, in the official Windows Phone app store. The only problem was that Kaspersky didn't produce a version of their anti-malware for the Windows phone. The app was a fake that did nothing after being purchased.[99]

The fake Kaspersky product wasn't the only one either. The same developers made fake versions of numerous other security products, including versions of Eset, Avira, and Norton Security. Likewise, they created fake copies of browsers that again did nothing and came with a price tag.

It isn't only fake Windows Phone apps either. In April 2014, an anti-virus app called Virus Shield made its way onto the official Google Play app store. It was downloaded over 10,000 times and reached the #1 new paid app position. Android users gave Virus Shield a 4.7 out of 5 rating. The only problem was that Virus Shield did nothing apart from turn a red x to a tick on the screen. (I assume to show the system was safe from any virus or malware.) It was a total fake app that couldn't detect anything, scan for malware, or provide any protection. How it managed to get on Google Play and get rated so highly doesn't say much about Goggle's app store checking process or the Android users who paid for and rated it.

Malicious Mobile Apps

The malicious mobile app market is a broad category. Depending on who you talk to, it includes: adware, rootkits, spyware, trojans, worms, fake installers, ransomware, and exploit kits, all with multiple varieties and versions.

For the sake of clarity I'm going to further break this down into two broad groups of software, namely malware and grayware:

Malware are programs deliberately written to cause harm and steal data from victims. Malware can either be hidden inside other applications or downloaded in the background onto the device. Malware includes trojans of all kinds, worms, rootkits, viruses, and spyware. More than half of the mobile malware is financially motivated and includes banking application trojans, ransomware, and SMS trojans.

Mobile Spyware Applications

Another problem area is mobile spyware. This involves mobile apps accessing other areas of your phone that have nothing to do with them. This is one way malicious apps can take over a mobile device or simply skim off private data. They could access your camera, microphone, GPS, NFC, and contacts when they don't need access to any of these. Most of this goes on in the background with consumers unaware that the apps they have downloaded are in fact stealing data or spying on them.

An infamous example being the Android "Brightest Flashlight" mobile app that turned your phone into a flashlight. This free download that was stealing and selling user location data in the background. The FTC stepped in and fined the developers, but not before tens of millions of users had downloaded the mobile app.[100]

A trick used by cyber criminals and unethical app developers alike is to start out with a useful benign mobile app. However, once downloaded and given access to all areas and features of the mobile phone, an update is pushed out, which when installed takes advantage of its unlimited access to steal data or monitor the owner of the phone.

The list of hidden, unauthorized features malicious apps use to steal data includes:

- Collecting **SMS messages** and sending them back to the app developer.

- Collecting **call log details**, such as data and time of your calls, the numbers called, and sending the data back to the app developer.

- Stealing your **photos** by sending copies back to the app developer.

- Stealing your **phone numbers** by sending a copy of all your contacts from your address book back to the app developer.

- Stealing **personal account details** including password and login details for any applications you access from your mobile phone.

- **Recording your calls** and/or conversations by accessing the microphone.

- Collecting **calendar events** and sending the details to the app developer.

Grayware is used as a catchall term to describe applications that degrade the performance of the device they are installed on, and often introduce security risks or impact the user's privacy. Although not totally malicious, once installed grayware can change settings, install bookmarks and unwanted icons, and generally be difficult to remove. Many free apps will often conceal grayware of some sort. Some users will intentionally download grayware applications, unaware of the annoying and potentially dangerous hidden code that it contains.

Another term often used for grayware is PUP (Potentially Unwanted Program) or PUA (Potentially Unwanted Application).

Examples of grayware would be: adware, fake programs, fraudulent dialers, RATs (remote access tools), redirection code, nuisance toolbars, and scareware.

Adware
Adware is a form of grayware. Adware is used to deliver obtrusive advertising or to connect the user to an advertising network. Typical examples of the behavior from devices infected with adware and spyware include:

- Continually displaying pop-up and banner ads while the mobile device is in use. Some ads may be linked back to additional unrelated advertising or malware-infected websites.

- Inserting ads in the SMS inbox. Ad embedded links lead to more advertising or malware-infected sites.

- Modifying and adding browser bookmarks that lead to advertising or malware-infected sites.

- Creating and adding icons onto the device screen, which lead to advertising or malware-infected sites.

- Redirecting the web browser to websites not asked for.

- Altering search results.

- Playing audio ads that disrupt phone calls.

If any of these activities are observed on your phone or tablet, it's a good indication you have adware installed. Often adware can be combined with other grayware or malware to produce new annoyances and security threats. All adware should be removed as soon as it's discovered on any device.

Mobile Application Privacy Policies

It's imperative to check the privacy policy of mobile apps. Ideally this should be before downloading them. However, the problem is that the majority of apps (in both Google Play and the Apple App store) don't link the app privacy policy to the store listing. So for many apps, both paid and free, there is no way to check the privacy policy without downloading the app first. You might not know if there is a privacy policy in place at all!

Even when mobile apps do include a link to a privacy policy, it doesn't actually mean the privacy policy will be there. During research for this book, I clicked on numerous privacy policy links of products in the Apple App store that didn't actually lead to a privacy policy.

So there are many apps that deal with highly personal data. Yet they don't disclose what data is being collected or how that data will be used or whom it will be shared with. So if your privacy is important to you, there are some apps you have to pass by and not download, or remove them if you already have it on your device.

Even where there is a clearly written privacy policy, the answers are not very clear. There are dozens of health apps tracking weight, medication apps tracking the dose etc., blood pressure tracking apps, mood tracker apps, ovulation and menstruation tracking apps, sleep pattern tracking apps, and personality profiles—all collecting very personal private information that is tied directly back to an individual. Likewise, financial apps track budgets, bills to pay, check printing apps— all collecting financial information from individuals. Where does all this information end up? And what do the companies do with it?

Some of the privacy policies are horrible and not in the user's favor. They will tell you right up front that they intend to share your personal information with their third party partners. Then they inform you that you need to read the privacy policy of the third parties. And by the way, they are not responsible for how their third party partners handle your data!

Mobile Applications: Take Action Steps

General mobile application security and privacy best practice:

- **App stores**. Only download software from the official Apple, Google, and Microsoft mobile app stores. (Especially in the case of Android.) There are numerous alternative third party app stores full of malware and grayware-laden apps, waiting to catch unlucky users. Even though many apps on the official app stores have bad privacy stealing features, at least some level of checking has been applied before they are allowed onto the stores. Alternative app stores often have copies of paid for original apps at cheaper prices or offer them for free. That's a good sign they contain code you don't want on your mobile device.

- **Update Apps**. Mobile apps, just like any other software, are often released with vulnerabilities that need to be patched with updates. Running unpatched mobile apps opens security holes into your smartphone. You need to keep all the apps updated that you use on a regular basis.

- Watch your **bank and credit card statements** for any unauthorized charges. If you notice any errors, be quick to challenge illegitimate charges.

Mobile Application Security and Privacy Tools:

Mobile application permission monitoring
Mobile apps accessing data they shouldn't is a major concern on smartphones and tablets.

- Be very cautious before downloading mobile apps and always read what permissions the app is requesting access to. For instance, if the app wants to access your microphone or camera and it doesn't need to, don't download the app. If anything looks suspicious, leave it off your device.

- **SnoopWall Privacy App**
(http://www.snoopwall.com/consumer/) is a useful free tool to install, which is available for Android and Windows. (The iOS version is still in development.) SnoopWall will find all apps which are spying on you, help uninstall any bad apps, audit your banking apps for security flaws, and show you which apps are accessing your webcam, GPS, Bluetooth, WiFi, NFC, and microphone.

Secure Mobile Web Browsing Tools

- **Disconnect Premium** (https://disconnect.me) will block ad networks from tracking and displaying ads when using apps and your mobile browser. If you don't use F-Secure Freedome, Disconnect Premium includes a VPN to protect your online activity and hide your location from websites and trackers.

Mobile Anti-malware

In general be very cautious when choosing any mobile anti-malware apps from companies you haven't heard of. Vendors such as F-Secure, LookOut, McAfee (Intel), Webroot, Sophos, Trend, and Zone Alarm (Check Point) are all leaders in cyber security. You can trust that their solutions won't contain malware and will do a good job of protecting your devices. Many currently offer free anti-malware software for mobile devices.

- Many of the security products recommended in this book provide free coverage for smartphones. For instance, **Webroot SecureAnywhere** (my choice of complete anti-malware solution) covers multiple devices including Android and iOS phones and tablets.

- An alternative all round Android mobile app is **ZoneAlarm Capsule** http://www.zonealarm.com/capsule/index.htm from Check Point. This useful protection contains an anti-malware solution, mobile app permission monitor, and a VPN.

- If you simply want a standalone mobile anti-malware solution, there are several good choices of free products including **Avast!** Mobile Security, **Avira** Anti-virus Security, **McAfee** Anti-virus & Security, and **Trend Micro** Anti-virus. They can be found on the Apple App store or Google Play.

Smartphones have transformed the way we communicate. It's unfortunate that they are so unsecure and have been turned into tracking devices. It's a good thing that there is a growing number of privacy and security apps. But be warned because there are also fake security apps, which might look like the real deal, so get the facts before you download. By using the solutions highlighted you will be able to secure your devices and communicate in private.

Chapter 11

Social Media Privacy and Security

"Every CEO of a social network should be required to use the default privacy settings for all of their accounts on the service."
Anil Dash, technologist and blogger

From humble beginnings, social media has changed society in many ways. Each day multiple millions of users use their favorite social media applications and forums. With social media they connect, share information, see what others are doing, watch videos, find out how to do stuff, look at photos, and post details of almost every part of their lives.

While social media really has made the world a smaller place, it's also made the mass collection of personal information so easy. That's why Google, Facebook, Flickr, Tumbler, Instagram, LinkedIn, Pinterest, YouTube, Twitter, and the entire host of social media, photo sharing, and other web forums are NOT free to use. You PAY for them by contributing your personal data and photos. These are then treated as a product to be packaged and sold for profit. Additionally, there is ample evidence that national intelligence and law enforcement agencies of all types regularly tap into and use social media to conduct background checks and build profiles on private citizens. Many times they are simply collecting information because they can.

Teenagers are, of course, the most connected segment of society today. In many ways, social media and mobile devices have replaced physically hanging out together, and distance has been removed. In our current world, it doesn't matter what time of day or night it is, if they are awake, teens and young adults tend to be online texting, messaging, or sharing video clips of some kind.

So while technology has benefitted teenagers in many ways, it has also exposed their private lives. Society has never had to deal with this issue before. As executive chairman of Google, Eric Schmidt commented on teenagers over sharing personal information, *"We have never had a generation with a full photographic, digital record of what they did."*

As far as privacy goes, many teenagers and young adults act as if they don't care who knows what about them. Many social media, data brokers, and other business interests have taken their actions as an indication that they can collect everything that is posted and use this data anyway they want.

After over-sharing for several years, it seems at least some teenagers and millennials are finally waking up to that fact they have over paid for "free" social media usage. In June 2015, a Pew Research report showed that 75% of young people are in fact very concerned about their privacy and 55% realize they have given too much data away.[101]

It's not only teenagers who are active on social media. Increasingly older citizens are also using social media to connect and re-connect with far-flung family members. They are considered one of the fastest growing segments on sites like Facebook and of course, many over-share information and treat social media as if it were private email.

Social Media as Public Records

Freedom of speech is not unlimited. Social media networks of today will be the public records of tomorrow. Increasingly, companies, organizations, and government departments are all monitoring and collecting public information posted on social media.

The data you post today may very well be used to determine if you qualify for a loan, what rate you should be paying, if you have any pre-existing medical conditions and should be paying higher insurance premiums, or if you should be denied a job or government benefit. Many companies actively monitor their staff members to see what they say about the company online. Likewise, universities and colleges monitor students online and particularly the behavior of athletes.

Securing Yourself on Social Media

The information that you share in online chat forums, blogs, social media, and other online forums, no matter how personal, once shared it becomes public information. So be careful what you post online, as once it's out there you can have no expectation of privacy or confidentiality with respect to that data.

Yet today people still share everything imaginable. In our social media obsessed culture, we tend to think the world needs to know all the details of our private life. Going on vacation? Post away and let everyone know you won't be at home! From having a meal to doing something crazy, it all needs a photo or video post for the world to see. Without posting an update, the event doesn't feel real to many. Okay, we all like to hear news from our close friends and family, but it's probably safe to say, social media has made sharing just a bit too easy and most people could probably learn some boundaries to their online behavior and share less.

We even have criminals tweet and post photos on social media sites showing the spoils of their crimes. Yes, Facebook is one of the first places criminal investigators look because they know many criminals post revealing details.

Terrorist organizations use social media as well. To share their messages of hate, to recruit, and to research and identify targets.

211

Recently, Twitter shut down numerous Jihad sites.[102] In response, the Jihadists threatened to behead Dick Costolo, the then CEO of Twitter. At the same time, ISIS and other radicals have used their online social media presence to call for targeted accounts against leaders of U.S. corporations including investor Warren Buffet among others.

Privacy for Children on Social Media Sites

Apart from teenagers and young adults over-sharing online, studies have shown that parents are in fact one of the biggest vectors through which personal information about children under age 13 is leaked.[103] Parents with public access wide-open to their accounts often post photos of their children, and give out their names and ages online. In one study conducted by researchers at the New York University Polytechnic School of Engineering and NYU Shanghai, it was shown how parent's poor privacy habits on Facebook and Instagram allowed researchers to identify children online by name and age, and then link the children to a home address. Law enforcement in numerous countries across Europe and the U.S. have called for parents to be more responsible in sharing children's photos online. At least limit post viewing to friends only.

Cyber Criminals on Social Media

Cyber criminals also love social media and are as savvy as any teenager using it. Fraudulent social media profiles are the new standard for launching cyber attacks. It's almost too easy today. Looking to steal from a business, they simply head on over to LinkedIn and find dozens of people at the company they wish to target. Alternatively they look for friends or a supplier to the target a so called "gatekeeping friend" tactic. Next they crosscheck on Facebook, Instagram, and Twitter to find out interests that they can use to start a social engineering attack. Lastly, they friend their victim using a carefully created false account. Never has it been easier for cyber criminals to find people, research them, and plan a targeted attack.

The guidelines for all who work in a business are simple. Restrict all social media posts to friends only, and don't post business related information on your personal social media accounts. Don't accept friend requests from those you don't know. Be alert to any strange requests you receive, as you have no idea who is really behind a social media profile. It's amazing how quickly normal, rational people become when a good-looking stranger sends them an online friend or connect request!

Delete Old Accounts

Don't forget old forums and social media accounts you may no longer use. Just because you may no longer use a platform or web forum doesn't mean your data isn't still out there and can't be found.

I'm not talking about old Usenet and bulletin board systems which are probably long gone by now, but web forums you may have forgotten like dating sites, MySpace, Friendstar, and others. If you opened accounts and had a personal profile, the data is probably still there. The same is true with old photo sharing accounts like Photobucket, Flickr, and others.

Social Media Best Practices: Take Action Steps

- If you care about your privacy, use a fake profile: fake user name, date of birth, place of birth, and fake answers to security questions *(See section on misinformation strategy).*

- If you require a phone number to sign up (some services want to send a sign-up verification code), use an app like **Burner** (burnerapp.com), as a temporary number. This will hide your real number.

- Use a VPN when signing up for any social media account. This will hide your true location as most accounts capture the IP address when you sign up.

- Use a strong unique password, supplied by a password manager, for each separate social media account. *(See section on passwords for more details on setting and maintaining strong passwords.)*
  - Hackers and cyber criminals spend their days and nights looking for ways to break into systems. Bypassing weak social media logins is easy for a skilled hacker.

- Change the default privacy settings from public to friends only. *(See specific privacy and security enhancing details under each individual social media section later in this chapter.)*

- Increase privacy settings to limit the audience for images of your children; make Instagram accounts private; think twice before sharing potentially embarrassing images of children; avoid sharing a child's name or location.

- Log out of accounts when you are finished. This prevents anyone else who has access to your device accessing your account. Plus it reduces the amount of online tracking.

- Be aware of applications that ask you to use your Facebook login to gain access. Some may be legitimate. However, they will share what you do on their platform with Facebook (so more collection of your data). They can be scams like UnfriendAlert (which promises to alert you when someone unfriends you on Facebook). This application asks for your Facebook login details so it can steal them from you and installs malicious software on your system.

o   As a simple rule, you shouldn't use your Facebook login details on any other website.

Facebook

Facebook is a behemoth and dwarfs all other social media platforms. Facebook claims to have over 1.49 billion active accounts, with nearly 1 billion of those active daily. In context that means approximately one in seven people on the planet access Facebook daily. Of the total, 87% or 1.25 billion, use Facebook on their mobile devices.

If you have a Facebook account, then Facebook knows A LOT about you. Apart from all the personal information you gave them when you signed up for the their "free" service, Facebook watches and gathers information from everything you do—both on their platform and when you are off their site and looking at other websites.

In 2009 when Facebook introduced their "like" button, they created an instant new way for users to signal their approval and interest in brands, topics, and issues. All "likes" are added to further refine user profiles.

Facebook claims they don't sell your personal information to other outside information data brokers. (At least not at this time, but never say never.) They keep it for their own marketing purposes in order to target ads tailored to your specific tastes—all based on the information they have gathered about you.

However, in March 2015 Facebook started to allow some data-analysis firms to harvest their databases on behalf of their clients. Mostly large consumer focused brands such as General Mills and Procter & Gamble. They are starting to look through user posts for key words related to the consumer brands. At this time, the marketing firms are said to have no access to actual personal identifiable information.[104] However, this could signal a change in direction for the social media giant. Either way, you know that whatever you post on Facebook and other social forums will be collected and turned into money.

The social media advertising market was reported to be worth $16 billion in 2014. For Facebook in 2014, their average revenue per user (ARPU) worldwide based on advertising and payments was around $2. (More in the USA and Canada but less in Europe, Asia, and the rest of the world).[105] That's a lot of money, especially when it comes in year after year. Hence you can understand why Facebook is so focused on gathering personal data and accurately profiling its ever-growing user base.

Facebook Privacy

Many who are concerned about preserving their privacy, skip using Facebook altogether. Facebook is certainly useful to keep up with friends and family. Especially if you have a far-flung network, usage needs to be balanced with the resulting loss of privacy. Facebook has faced numerous complaints from its user base regarding its handling of personal information. A report in August 2015 looking at Facebook's ever-changing privacy policies from 2005 to 2015, concluded that Facebook has (with the exception of a few overhauls) continued to get worse at protecting the privacy of its users data each year.[106]

Some examples: In 2011, Facebook was forced by the FTC into agreeing on better privacy protection. They could not just make unilateral changes to their policies and expose user's previously private information. (Which seems reasonable when they hold so much personal information in trust.) In addition, Facebook agreed to annual independent privacy audits to ensure it doesn't misuse the huge amount of personal information it collects. While the FTC agreement was a step in the right direction in terms of protecting user data, many privacy concerns still remain.

Since then Facebook has faced numerous other privacy missteps that have kept their legal team busy. In 2013 they were forced in a class action settlement to reverse course. They had started using, without permission, personal images and names of users to promote products and services to their friends as if they were personal endorsements.

In late 2014, Facebook faced another class action lawsuit over unauthorized scanning of private messages on their platform. And the list goes on. In Europe where privacy laws are a lot stricter than in the USA, Facebook has faced numerous legal challenges from both private users as well as national regulators.

One of the biggest concerns with Facebook and the protection of data is that many users themselves are not aware how exposed their data really is. Too many people post photos and information on Facebook (and other social media and web forums) as if they were having a private conversation with close friends. In my own circle of friends and family I've asked, "Who can see your images and posts?" Too many times I've seen the look of disbelief when they realize they are sharing everything they post on Facebook with the whole world. In late 2014 Facebook finally reworked their over 9,000-word privacy policy into everyday English and started an initiative called Privacy Basics. With tutorials, Privacy Basics attempted to educate users on better use of protecting who can actually see what when they post, comment, and like on Facebook. However, Facebook continues to face criticism that it continually pushes the boundaries on privacy.

You may make a qualified decision that you are prepared to pay for the convenience of Facebook's platform with your personal information. Make no mistake, while you can lock down some privacy settings to restrict some information, Facebook still tracks your every click, like, tag, and who your friends are. Even if you make all the posts on your own page "Friends only," when you post on a friend's wall, if their settings are different, your posting can be seen.

In the end it doesn't matter how secure or what privacy settings you chose, there will always be a way to find data and identify individuals. For example, in August 2015, a software engineer showed how he was able to exploit a flaw in Facebook's privacy settings to obtain cellphone numbers of thousands of people. He then linked these back to identify specific people's profiles and gathered the user's Facebook ID, locations, images, and more.[107] The scary part of this story is the company that found the security hole wasn't even a cyber security or hacker group. They are SEO (search engine optimization) experts and they weren't looking for flaws—they found this by mistake!

The point is, when using Facebook and any other social media platform, don't write or post anything you want to keep confidential and be prepared for your private posts and profile to come to light.

Facebook Audit

If you are currently a Facebook user and you want to see how much information Facebook has gathered on you, you can start with a personal audit. To do so, use the "download my data feature."

Facebook will email a secure link to the email you have listed on your Facebook account. This link takes you to a page to download an archive of your Facebook activities and data.

The archive Facebook sends you contains all your data neatly broken down by category as follows:

- Profile (your email, birthday, relationships, all your likes—music, movies, television shows, your favorite teams and athletes, and any groups you belong to)
- Contact information
- Wall (everything you have written—status updates, likes, what you have rated, what you have shared)

- Photos (your profile photos, your timeline photos, and all your cover photos)
- Videos (any videos you have posted)
- Friends (lists of all your friends, your sent and received friend requests, and any removed friends)
- Messages (copies of all your personal messages)
- Pokes
- Events
- Settings (all notification settings and privacy settings)
- Security (all account status changes, account activity showing recorded IP addresses, browser, system, and cookie information)
- Mobile settings

Your Privacy on Facebook

If you want to keep your Facebook presence, the following alternatives will give you some privacy from those not listed as your friends.

What's my name?

Facebook is not a bank or government department so if you don't yet have a Facebook account and want one, you are under no legal obligation to use your real name, birthdate, and other personal information. Yes, Facebook asks for it and you have to follow their rules, but it's not a legal, Federal, or state requirement so you can make up any name and birthdate. That way you can be on Facebook and keep up with friends. The downside is unless friends know your fake name, they won't be able to find you, which of course might be okay with you. You do run the risk of being kicked off Facebook under their no-fake profile rule if Facebook figures out your name is not real. Compared to the risk of losing as much personal information that Facebook gathers, I would suggest it's worth the small inconvenience and risk.

Using your Facebook login on other Websites

As a best practice, you should not use your Facebook credentials ("use my Facebook details") to login into any third party application, either on the web or via a mobile app. Doing so not only allows Facebook to gather more information on your web usage, but it also exposes you to privacy risks.

There is a known vulnerability in the mobile Facebook app login that is used by third party applications on both Apple iOS and Android devices. This vulnerability is called Facebook Social Login Session Hijacking and exploits the Facebook Access Token (FAT). The majority of third party mobile apps that allow users to login using their mobile Facebook login credentials are vulnerable to this exploit. Social session hijacking can give an attacker access to take over a private Facebook account.

Leaving Facebook

If you have a FB account and want to leave or delete it, there are two different ways to do so. You can either temporally deactivate your account or permanently delete it.
- o   Deactivate, which is a temporary shutdown.
- o   Permanent delete, which erases all your data. Facebook says this can take up to 90 days to remove all your data, posts, and photos from all backups.

To do either go to: Settings, Security, Deactivate, or Delete my account.

LinkedIn

LinkedIn is a business focused social networking site. It's the third largest social network behind Facebook and Twitter with over 350 million users. LinkedIn is the largest source of business resumes for networkers and recruiters. Unfortunately, the same information can be a treasure trove for social engineers as well.

LinkedIn Security Settings

To change LinkedIn security settings, login. Under "Account & Settings" choose "Privacy & Settings." You will have to enter your email and password a second time to enter the settings menu.

Choose the "Account tab" and then "Manage security settings." Next click the box "secure connection" which will enable HTTPS while you are on LinkedIn.

Then choose "Two-step verification for sign-in" to add a second step pass code when logging into your LinkedIn account. By adding a mobile phone number, LinkedIn will send you a passcode to complete your login.

LinkedIn Privacy Settings

LinkedIn has made progress in their privacy settings since founder Reid Hoffman arrogantly stated that "privacy is for old people" in Davos, Switzerland in 2011.

Now it is possible to manage your privacy on LinkedIn by changing your public profile. This determines who can see your photo, work resume, and other information you have entered by searching for you via online search engines. You are either able to totally opt out or choose only the parts of your profile you wish to display.

To change LinkedIn security settings, login. Under "Account & Settings" choose "Privacy & Settings." You will have to enter your email and password a second time to enter the settings menu.

On the "Profile tab" choose "Change your profile photos and visibility." Using the large "View profile" button next to your image, select "Manage public profile settings."

Opting out of having your details appearing in Google searches is easy. Simply choose "Make my public profile visible to no-one." This doesn't stop anyone from seeing your details once they are logged into LinkedIn, but it does stop your LinkedIn profile from showing up in public search results.

Chapter 12

Securing the Internet-of-Things

"The Internet-of-Things is happening. The world is becoming hyper-connected, whether we want it or not - security be damned!"

John Matherly, Shodan ®, IoT search engine creator

Depending on whom you listen to, the Internet-of-Things (IoT) is either a bright exciting technology future full of "smart" objects that will make our lives easier, or it's an unsecure nightmare of connected vulnerable devices. The truth is probably somewhere in the middle.

The IoT is basically an Internet-of-sensors. From new wearable healthcare devices to thousands of different smart home devices and appliances, everything will be connected and accessible online. The IoT is already in the process of adding millions of connected devices to the web. Smaller sensors, massive bandwidth, cheap storage, and huge amounts of capital investment are driving IoT innovation. As consumers are sold on the benefits (real and perceived), adoption will be rapid. Everything is going online whether it makes sense or not.

The next major step for IoT devices will be connecting with so-called smart city infrastructure. Consumer-owned portable smart devices and cars will interact with autonomous infrastructures such as roadways, parking garages, buildings, and public places. Embedded sensors will gather and exchange information with our devices. As the level of data sharing increases, new privacy and data security challenges will be raised.

International research group Gartner estimates there were 3.8 billion connected devices at the end of 2014. This included: smart cars, door locks, thermostats, smoke detectors, streetlights, heart monitors, wind turbines, smart trains, and more. They see this number increasing rapidly to over 25 billion devices by 2020 with the average modern household containing hundreds of smart connected sensors.[108] Others, including John Chambers, CEO of Cisco, believe the number of IoT connected devices will be closer to 50 billion, all sending and receiving data about us and our environment to the cloud and to other smart connected devices. As databases overflow with new data from reporting smart devices, the IoT is introducing a privacy nightmare.

The Internet-of-Hacked Things

"Connected devices invite attackers, making the Internet-of-Things a worrisome trend from a security perspective."

Ted Harrington, Executive Partner, Independent Security Evaluators

IoT devices are being rapidly developed. While manufacturers are now starting to be aware of security issues, there still doesn't appear to be enough action taking place. The issue is very simple. Household appliances, cars, and building product companies are not experienced technology vendors and it costs money to add security. There is a worldwide shortage of highly skilled cyber security professionals. It's obvious from many early IoT products that cyber security wasn't a top priority during design. At almost every hacker and cyber security conference, numerous proof-of-concept IoT exploits are highlighted or demonstrated, proving that many systems are far from secure. The FBI also recently issued an IoT cyber security public service announcement in an attempt to educate users and vendors to the cyber security risks.[109]

In a real-world example that hit headlines recently, two security researchers demonstrated that while they were sitting on their couch they could hack a new Jeep, taking over its Internet connected steering, braking, and transmission systems and take it off the road without the driver's permission. In another connected car hack, researchers remotely turned off the air bags in a new Audi. Hopefully, examples like this will reinforce the message to manufacturers and will cause them to be cautious before adding an IP address to all and every devices. At the very least they need to concentrate on how to secure the connection. Currently, many IoT devices that are open to the Internet by default are being sold without any warning notices. Connections are mostly unencrypted and with no authentication options at all.[110]

Numerous technology vendors are ringing alarm bells in an attempt to ensure more security is added. According to cyber security firm F-Secure, up to 70% of current IoT connected devices already have serious vulnerabilities. Hewlett Packard's research points out that the vast majority of IoT devices are sending unencrypted data, and most don't require robust passwords. Both of these issues make them easy to hack and leak personal data.[111] Leading technology research group IDC goes even further predicting that within 2 years, up to 90% of IoT networks will suffer security breaches—so the future of connected devices looks to be even more unsecure than computer systems of the past. As evidence, security firm Symantec has spoken of computer worms that target devices running embedded Linux, which would include many IoT devices.[112]

One of the most damning reports has been from Proofpoint. In early 2014 they stated that they detected a spam-sending botnet that contained approximately 100,000 home connected IoT devices. This included televisions, multimedia centers, and home networking routers.[113] In essence all 100,000 IoT devices were already compromised and infected.

IoT Hacks will Focus on Money

Most hackers are only interested in making money. So attacks against IoT devices and even Internet connected smart cars are only likely to occur when the attackers can profit from the hack. For instance, hacking your household devices to break them makes little sense to a hacker. But hacking your Internet connected front door to open it and disable your home security system so onsite thieves can enter is worthwhile for criminals.

Likewise, while disabling the brakes or taking over the steering of a car makes for great news headlines, this doesn't make a lot of sense as a regular hack, unless of course the hackers are getting paid to harm or kill you. It's far more likely that they will want to unlock the car security system, start the engine, and disable the GPS in order to steal the vehicle. Another scenario would be infecting the car with a ransomware trojan which would require a Bitcoin payment before the car could be accessed or driven. These are the types of IoT attacks we can expect to see in the not too distant future.

Mobile Devices are the Gateway

The majority of IoT connected devices are controllable via the web from smartphone based mobile apps. As the IoT continues to expand, many security researchers are predicting that controlling mobile apps will become a focus for malware developers. Many mobile devices are vulnerable to exploits due to a combination of weak built-in security and over-trusting users. The key to securing mobile apps is for users to install mobile anti-malware, encrypt data on their mobile devices, and keep apps and mobile operating systems updated. *(See Chapter Seven: "Getting Your Mobile Devices under Control" for more info on securing smartphones and tablet computers.)*

In the short term, there will be many more unsecure applications and devices that most consumers will never securely configure. Hopefully in the long run, manufactures will bake in enough security to keep devices from being compromised. Maybe there could be a firewall/gateway security appliance to protect all your connected home appliances? In the meantime, the IoT has the potential to be a house of insecurity and privacy horrors.

Obsolescence

Another big IoT security problem will be that of obsolescence. Computers are replaced every 2-3 years, and most smartphones every 2 years. However, we expect our household appliances to last for far longer, sometimes 8 to10 years before being replaced. What will happen when vendors don't keep up with firmware updates or security patches? Or IoT devices are so old they can no longer be patched? The answer as we know from today's computing systems is that unpatched, vulnerable systems are hacked. And this opens holes into any attached devices, which may contain sensitive data.

Shodan

As if the thought of millions of unpatched and barely secure home-connected devices isn't enough to concern you, there is Shodan, the search engine that will find them all for you. While traditional search engines like Google and Bing find websites, Shodan searches for and finds devices. Once it finds a device, it indexes it by numerous categories including country, device type, brand, operating systems, etc. So anyone wanting to find unpatched Internet connected webcams, thermostats, smart TVs, routers, or other IoT devices can make use of the filters, providing detailed lists of specific devices.[114] Smart hackers love the Shodan search platform.

The Connected Home—Sensors Everywhere

The ultimate end game for most IoT manufactures is a fully automated and everything-connected smart home.

One of early poster children for this vision is the Nest learning thermostat from Google. Thermostats are responsible for more energy consumption in the average home than the lights, TV, computers, and microwave combined. The Nest device, which can be controlled from a smartphone, "learns" the home occupants' schedule and programs itself accordingly. Nest devices are compelling, boasting they can save most users up to 20% on energy costs, effectively paying for themselves.

The concept of the smart home is more of the same:

- Cameras at the door to identify who is arriving with automatic entry for members of the household.
- Sensors in door handles to take your temperature and heart rate. All family member's health information displayed on monitors inside the house.
- Smart kitchen appliances that detect your weight and offer meal options based on your health, weight body data.
- Smart air conditioners sense when a room is occupied. When it's not, they change the rate of airflow to save electricity.
- Smart, voice activated entertainment systems that display on multiple wall screens and follow you as you move from room to room.

All smart devices are being controlled by apps on your smartphone and sending feedback on usage to the cloud. Consumers will flock to them as a way to save energy, to improve security, and their lifestyle.

Connected Home Hacks

Already white-hat hackers have demonstrated connected home hacks.

In August 2014 at the Black Hat security conference, Google's Nest thermostats were shown to be vulnerable to physical hacking with security researchers "jail breaking" them in 10–15 seconds. The researchers from University of Central Florida believe they could perform the same hacks remotely, as most smart devices are nodes on a network. The hack was basically an indication to point out that a lot more security needs to be added to most IoT devices.

Keyless Locks

Keyless entry into homes is another example. Instead of using a traditional key to open a door lock, either a smartphone or a USB type key fob are used. This is similar to keyless systems currently used to unlock high-end cars. While convenient for car owners, smart thieves have found ways to bypass the built-in security and can easily steal them. This is much to the dismay of some luxury Range Rover owners in London, who have been denied insurance because their cars are considered too easy to steal.[115]

The same sort of thing will happen with keyless doors in homes. Thieves working in teams will hack the locks and gain entry. It's really no different to picking a non-digital lock. However, if the smart lock is accessible via the Internet, the hacker could be located anywhere in the world, with a local accomplice waiting on site to enter the premises as soon as the smart lock is opened.

Security Cams

Home security cams, baby monitors, nanny cams, whatever you call them, they all do the same thing. Users install them to allow for remote checking of their home, baby, children, pets, or simply for additional home security. The problem is too many people forget to change the default factory passwords. So anyone who knows how to use a search engine to search for devices can find Internet attached home security cameras. By using the known default password, they can login and use the camera to spy on whomever the device is facing.

In November 2014, a Russian web forum listing many thousands of non-secure Internet attached cameras made news headlines around the world. Anyone could visit the website and choose a camera to view live video streaming of unsuspecting individuals. Many of these cameras were positioned in private areas like living rooms and bedrooms! In addition to the unfiltered live streaming, the website provided the camera's exact GPS details, plus the postcode and time stamp of the video. The website even went so far as to claim that it wasn't hacking, because they simply used the default passwords for the devices. In their opinion, it was the user's own fault that they were now streaming their lives online!

Numerous similar stories often pop-up in the news media of baby monitors being accessed and used to creep parents out.

IoT Security: Take Action Steps

- Always make security part of your purchasing criteria for any smart connected device. Paying extra for a more secure product will be worth it.

- Change the default factory password on all devices.

- Keep all devices updated. Install all manufacturer firmware and software security updates.

- As smart devices are connected to home and office WiFi networks, make sure you have configured them securely. *(For more information on WiFi security, see chapter 8.)*
    - Set a secure password on all WiFi gateways.
    - Change the name of your WiFi network so it doesn't reflect any personal details about you. Calling it Jones_home_WiFi is not a good idea. Instead something like

VX678GHI is more obscure and is not giving away any identifying information.

- o Wherever possible enable encryption. WPA2 is the most secure for WiFi connections.

- Mobile apps used to control IoT devices mean security on smartphones is a priority. *(For more information on mobile device security, see chapter 10.)*
  - o Add mobile anti-malware.
  - o Use a VPN when connecting to and controlling smart devices.
  - o Add all smartphones software upgrades.
  - o Be extra careful about adding new apps to your smartphone.

IoT Privacy: Take Action Steps

- Don't give your real name and information to IoT product manufacturers. Many will simply share your data with marketing firms and it will eventually end up in data broker databases.

- Read privacy policies. If you are not happy with the policy, return the product!

- Opt out of as much marketing and data sharing as possible. Most IoT firms collect data just because they can.

Wearable Technology

The market for wearable technology is going to be huge. As prices drop and the usefulness of applications increases, legions of consumers will join those who have already purchased them.

According to consulting group Accenture, 68% of 14 to 17 year olds worldwide say they plan to buy a smartwatch in the next 5 years.[116]

Over time, just as with smartphones, many will wonder how they lived without their wearable technology. George Orwell would be nodding his head and saying that he told us so!

Fitness Trackers

The market for wearable fitness and self-health monitoring is driving a technology start-up mini boom. The trend goes way beyond just fitness trackers and smartwatches. Numerous devices are available with sensors that monitor everything from blood pressure, the number of steps taken, distance covered every day, GPS routes, calories burned, and how long and how well the wearer sleeps. The next generation of wearable devices will measure far more.

New body monitoring applications are being rushed to market. So while most wearable devices have small amounts of storage, they upload all the collected data to application databases in the cloud. Just as with smartphones, many of the applications don't have much security at all. For example, submitting passwords in plain text. Considering the kind of data that health and fitness monitoring devices collect, this is not a good idea. Plus the old problem of users having the same password for multiple accounts applies. Once a username/password is stolen, it can be tried across multiple popular online services, normally with a high degree of success.

All fitness trackers contain a GPS and are vulnerable to location tracking, without the wearer knowing they are being tracked. Maybe the White House should pay close attention and inform the Secret Service as President Obama has been photographed wearing a Fitbit personal fitness tracker, which of course comes with a GPS and is traceable 24/7.

Privacy Concerns

When security researchers investigated how secure fitness trackers were, the first finding was that approximately half of all trackers don't even have privacy policies. Now, maybe they simply forgot about adding one (I'm being nice here). Or more likely it's because the vendors don't want to explain to users how much data they collect and what they do with it. Surveillance as a business model with the selling of personal data is just as widespread in the mobile device market.

Another concern to privacy advocates is that insurance companies are already taking notice of fitness trackers. Appirio,[117] a cloud vendor, was able to use fitness trackers to convince its health insurance company that their employees were exercising enough. This allowed them to negotiate lower insurance premiums. However, the potential downside of this type of arrangement is when health insurance companies start to make this kind of tracking a standard way of business for all their customers. What starts out as an option often ends up being compulsory. This level of access to real-time health data could allow insurers to bump up premiums of those with marginal conditions.

Fitness Trackers: Take Action Steps

While usability and appearance are clearly driving buying decisions, security should be added to that list. Until recently, no research group had done any comprehensive security comparison testing. Independent security researchers AV-Test, who have traditionally looked at anti-malware products, took it upon themselves to test the security readiness of nine popular fitness trackers. The results showed an amazing lack of thought around the issue of security by most vendors.

The clear winner in terms of security was the **Sony Smartband Talk**, followed by **Jawbone** and **Polar Loop**. Most vulnerable to hacking and leaking user data was the Acer Liquid Leap, followed by the Fitbit Charge. [118]

Privacy Policy

Another important consideration is only choosing a device that actually has a privacy policy. At least this shows that the vendor is more transparent about what they are doing with your data once it's been collected.

It's also important to keep firmware updated. Updates are normally released to close known vulnerabilities. So read the manual and see how the devices receive updates and apply any that the vendor issues.

It should go without saying, but choose and only use unique strong passwords for your online account. The easiest option is to use a password manager. *(See section on passwords for more details in Chapter 9.)*

Smartwatches

Smartwatches, just like all devices where we store personal data, are another security vector that hackers will attack.

According to HP, all current smartwatches are vulnerable to cyber attacks. [119] In early 2015, they ran 10 different manufacturer's products through typical cyber attacks. They found that all 10 exhibited at least one, and in most cases, many more serious security flaws.

It is acknowledged and understood that many are still early models, but manufacturers need to do a better job of adding security. All early adopters should be aware of this when making decisions about accessing personal, financial, or health data on a smartwatch. While smartwatch attacks are currently unheard of at this time, numerous security researchers have been demonstrating how they could occur.

In one such scenario, researchers showed how they could compromise a Samsung Gear Live smartwatch that was paired to a Google Nexus 4 smartphone by attacking the Bluetooth passcodes. [120]

In another case, Symantec demonstrated how an Android smartphone infected with mobile ransomware was able to infect a paired Android smartwatch. In order to add apps to smartwatches, they are paired to a smart device like a smartphone or tablet. If the smartphone or tablet becomes infected with malware, that malware could make the jump to the paired smartwatch. A factory reset may be the only option to remove malware from an infected smartwatch. Although as Symantec was able to demonstrate, ransomware malware could effectively block user access to the device. On some models of smartwatches, this would mean a factory reset would be impossible to perform.

Smartwatches: Take Action Steps

Most wearable technology opens the door to being tracked.

- Just as with other mobile devices, read product manuals to understand what privacy options are available and enable them. They probably won't be on by default.

- Be sure you fully understand what data is being collected and who has access to it. If it's only the vendor, that's probably not too bad. However, if the user agreement mentions sharing data with their "partners," your data will end up with some data broker.

As most wearables rely on smart devices to install apps, it's important to ensure any smartphones or tablets paired with smartwatches are fully patched with all security updates.

- As per advice on smartphones, only install apps from trusted sources like the official app stores for Android and iOS.

- Lastly, install security and anti-malware software on all smartphones and tablets. *(See section on mobile security and privacy in Chapter 10.)*

Summary

As wearable technology improves, it will become more seamlessly integrated into our everyday lives. Individuals will continue to acquire more wearable devices in order to track and monitor more areas of their lives including their health, fitness levels, and daily nutrition. Devices will also be used for other purposes such as entertainment, user authentication, and access control.

While the information gathered from a single device might be useful to the individual, device manufacturers and data brokers will be very motivated to access this data. It will help them tie the information back to larger personal profiles, giving a better understanding of their customers. It will assist them in the design of new products and services. The big challenge will be how to benefit from wearable technology without totally losing all privacy.

As people become more accustomed to being tracked by their wearable devices, even more invasive technology will start to be accepted. In the very near future, we will start to see a transition from wearable technology to embedded technology. Already companies are prototyping different types of implanted and digital tattoo technology.

236

Chapter 13

Tracking You Everywhere

"We are not yet at the point where we can take pictures of people on the street with our smartphones, identify them, and gain access to information about them. However, this reality may not be too far off and we can only imagine what that will do to our interactions, relationships, and how we conduct our lives. It will also make surveillance and facial recognition seem ordinary. If the use of this technology is normalized, no one will question it and put constraints around what it can be used for and by whom".[121]
Office of the Privacy Commissioner of Canada

In the offline world surveillance is increasing exponentially.

Surveillance Cameras

Surveillance cameras are a fact of modern life. They are literally everywhere. In most countries, law enforcement agencies are busy adding more surveillance cameras in public places. There really isn't much you can do to avoid them if you are out in public as they are seen by many as the best way to combat and catch terrorists like those that placed the bombs at the Boston marathon in 2013. By piecing together available CCTV footage, police were able to quickly identify the perpetrators and catch them. It's estimated that in the USA there are currently over 30 million surveillance cameras in public with more being added all the time. While some may question how effective CCTV is at actually stopping terrorist acts, that's beside the point. The future is full of more surveillance not less, and CCTV will be a big part of it.

Businesses likewise have numerous cameras at all entrances surveying those who enter their premises. Despite what is portrayed in TV dramas, in most cases law enforcement can't automatically access video footage from business video feeds. However, they can request it at any time. In the future, expect legislation allowing law enforcement to tap into private CCTV video feeds on demand.

In some countries with high crime, it's not only law enforcement and businesses using surveillance cameras. Criminals like surveillance cameras too. In Reynosa, Mexico and other areas, criminal gangs install their own surveillance cameras around the town to monitor law enforcement.[122]

Smart Cameras

Facial recognition software is improving all the time. Retailers are using systems to scan the faces of shoppers as they enter their stores and compare them to saved images of known shoplifters. In the near future, in-store retail facial recognition systems will present personalized offers to individual shoppers.

Additionally, smart checkout systems will "recognize" you. Perhaps in the future, using your face will automatically allow purchases to be charged to your linked credit card or bank account. From a convenience point, this will help reduce checkout times, and many will no doubt be pleased that the "system" recognized them. From the view of privacy, this technology is scary.

Facial Recognition

Facial recognition software is improving all the time. Simply by starting with an anonymous CCTV image of a person's face, facial recognition software can search through huge image databases to compare and find matches.

As an authentication method, facial recognition works particularly well. It provides 99% accuracy. Unlike numeric passwords and other personal information that can be changed by the user, facial features are fixed and can't be altered unless expensive surgery is involved. Retail outlets, public venues, and law enforcement are all increasing their use facial recognition technologies.

As a surveillance technology, however, facial recognition is one of the biggest threats to anonymity and privacy. In extending this technology, many retailers are testing ways to link captured facial images back to the vast stores of personal data. This would be the personal files and profiles that have been built by companies, social media, and data brokers. Once this becomes commonplace, it will be almost impossible to go to the mall or shop anonymously.

For that reason alone it's important to control, or at the very least have privacy guidelines around, the collection and usage of facial recognition software. This is especially important in retail malls and other public places. Otherwise, by deploying facial recognition systems, individuals will be picked out, identified, and cross-referenced with other data and social media sources, all without their knowledge or consent.

So while the benefits are easy to understand for businesses and law enforcement, worse case scenarios and abuses are also easy to imagine. This would include scenarios such as individuals being identified and targeted at demonstrations, outside churches, mosques, temples, treatment centers and clinics, bars, clubs, police stations, courts, and other sensitive areas.

How Facial Recognition Works
Everyone has a unique face with multiple distinguishable peaks and valleys that make up our facial features. These are

referred to as nodes or nodal points, and each face has approximately 80 of them. Facial recognition software uses these nodes to measure different parts of a face. These include measurements of eye sockets, nose, and chin—the width of the nose, the distance between the eyes, depth of eye sockets, shape of cheekbones, and length of jawline. These facial features don't change as we age, so it works well to identify individuals even using older photos or videos.

3D imaging is able to capture and build 3D images, which can be used even on images captured in poor light as they rely on comparing shapes to preform identification.

By matching enough facial nodes, facial recognition software can find matching images to verify the identity of individuals.

In law enforcement, facial recognition technology is used to identify people by matching images from arrests against databases of known felons. The matches in many cases consist of uploaded images on social media platforms, which are linked to profiles providing huge amounts of background personal information.

Privacy Concerns and Abuse

Facial recognition systems without the user's implicit consent brings up privacy and ethical issues and should be regulated to protect individual privacy. Unfortunately, as has been pointed out several times already, privacy is under attack in the United States and legislation is not keeping up. In recent meetings (February to June 2015) hosted by the Department of Commerce and aimed at providing a code of conduct for companies who use facial recognition technology, privacy campaigners couldn't even get the companies to agree to the most basic privacy protections.[123] [124] This can only point to a continued erosion of privacy in the name of profit by U.S. commercial entities. Currently in Europe, companies have to obtain the individual's permission before using facial recognition for commercial purposes. Two U.S. states, Illinois and Texas, have similar legislation.

Law enforcement has no such restrictions and is actively deploying facial recognition systems in airports, at border control points, and elsewhere. Additionally, most U.S. states load driver's license images into facial recognition systems for police to search.[125]

Facebook's usage of facial recognition software is a good example of privacy abuse. This matters as it's acknowledged that Facebook probably has the largest database collection of faceprints in the world. (Faceprint is the generic term for a person's recorded facial image, like fingerprint is the generic term for fingerprints.)

For years Facebook users have been adding their family photos and sharing them with friends. They then started to encourage users to add tags in order to identify people in their pictures. While everyone was busy uploading and tagging all their family and friends, Facebook went out and acquired facial recognition. They didn't tell anyone about it, they didn't ask for consent, and they didn't disclose what they intended to do with the data they were collecting. They simply crowd sourced the training and refining of their facial recognition system behind everyone's back. Then they introduced automatic image tag suggestions to further refine the system.

Facebook was able to get away with their facial recognition and tagging system in the USA, and many parts of the world where there were less strict personal privacy laws. However, in the European Union and Canada, they quickly ran into problems.

The European's opinion was something like, hey Facebook, forget it, you can't start building a database and naming everyone without their consent. Facebook fought but lost and had to close down those technologies in Europe.

- Factors that limit facial recognition include wearing sunglasses (or using dark tinted glasses indoors) and hats to shade your face from CCTV cameras.

- Do not give consent to retail companies to enroll you in their facial recognition systems.

- Don't use an actual photo of yourself as your profile photo on Facebook. Profile photos cannot be made private so everyone can view them.

- Delete any photos you find of yourself posted online by others. Ask your friends not to post your image without your okay.

- Prevent anyone from tagging you on Facebook.
  - If you are really serious about retaining your piracy, consider leaving Facebook altogether and avoid photo-sharing websites.

Sensors Everywhere—Mobile Location Analytics

Numerous public facilities such as malls, individual stores, airports, museums, and sports arenas are increasingly using Mobile Location Analytics (MLA) technology to better understand how people move around in their venues.

MLA technologies operate by detecting device wireless MAC or Bluetooth addresses—a 12-digit string of letters and numbers assigned to the device by its manufacturer.

If WiFi and Bluetooth services are enabled, smartphones continually broadcast their WiFi and Bluetooth addresses looking for networks and devices to connect to. Facilities using MLA sensors detect these addresses when nearby mobile devices broadcast them.

Once a device MAC address has been collected in a database, MLA technology makes it possible to identify and track individuals at the location and during repeat visits. Advocates of MLA solutions claim they help retailers improve store layouts and reduce checkout wait times. Critics of the technology usage are concerned about this data ending up in bloated data broker systems, which are used to profile users.

Privacy Concerns

Knowing where a particular person is, combined with CCTV technology, will allow facility operators to capture and assign a face to a particular mobile device. As image recognition technology improves, comparing CCTV captured images with personal facial images on social media profiles will allow customer profiling. Additionally, if stores collect wireless device MAC addresses, they will probably sell them to data brokers who will simply add them into your personal profile. This will allow you to be tracked and personally identified whenever you take your mobile device with you.

Mobile Location Analytics: Take Action Steps

If you don't wish venue operators to collect your WiFi MAC and Bluetooth device address, simply disable both before venturing out.

If you are using an iPhone with iOS 8, you already have some built-in protection against MLA technology. In order to protect the privacy of its users, Apple introduced random MAC addresses in iOS 8. Having MAC randomization means iPhones will be seen as a different device each time they are scanned.[126]

For Android devices, **Pry-Fi** from Dutch developer Chainfire offers similar capabilities by randomizing the WiFi MAC address.

An alternative to completely block all WiFi, cellular, and Bluetooth signals from reaching your smartphone is to place it inside a **Black Hole Faraday bag**. (*See section on RF blocking bags in Chapter 10.*)

Chapter 14

Get Involved

"You have to fight for your privacy or you will lose it."
Eric Schmidt, Executive Chairman, Google

Reading and following the steps outlined in this book will make you more informed and better protected than most people. However, that's not enough. To ensure your right to privacy doesn't go the way of the dodo, there is more you need to do.

Personal privacy and freedom of association and speech without being tracked are deeply personal for most people. The longer you delay taking privacy seriously, the more difficult it will be to get it back. Governments and big business will continue to over-reach into your private life.

Privacy is Not Dead Yet

When you grasp the fact that so much of our personal data has already been collected and logged by numerous companies, and that government and businesses constantly track us, it can be depressing. But fear not, privacy is not totally dead yet.

See that Others are Informed

One of the best actions you can do to ensure others are informed is to bring up the issue of privacy in conversations. Ask your friends and family if they know how to protect their personal information and if they know how to protect themselves online. *(If not, get them a copy of this book as a gift!)* Discuss social media privacy with your children and see they are protected. Privacy and online protection are vital issues and many are still ignorant of the facts. Having read this far, you are better informed than the majority of the population. Additionally, see you stay informed.

Don't Be a Passive Voter

The view that we need our politicians to understand is that just because companies and the government can track us and collect all our personal data, why should they?

It's a false ideology that to be secure we have to give up all privacy. Likewise, it's a lie that for big business to be profitable, they have to collect all our data without our consent. The fact is with better laws we can all—government, businesses, and individuals—have what we want:

- Government and law enforcement can track criminals and terrorists and not infringe on the rights of innocent citizens.

- Big business can collect data, advertise, and not treat us all like a product.

- Individuals can use all the modern technology we like without fearing we are being tracked and under surveillance by technology vendors and data brokers.

Updated Privacy Legislation

So if we can have these things, why don't we? Because in most cases, we haven't demanded it. We haven't put our point across in a loud enough voice, and we haven't made this a political issue yet. That's why don't we have better laws, like those in the European Union that give individuals (not companies) the right to own their own data. That's why we don't have common sense laws that allow law enforcement and the government to track the bad guys, but force them to delete or restrict the collection of data from the innocent.

The fact is we can have better personal privacy laws and we need them. It is too important for us to allow the continued abuse of our privacy.

Some examples of privacy related legislation we need to push our government representatives to pass include:

The Right to be Forgotten
The European Union has adopted "the right to be forgotten" Internet privacy legislation. [127] [128] This allows regular citizens to control their own data. They can ask search engines to remove links to data that is "inadequate, irrelevant, or no longer valid."

While this issue would require further debate and maybe some fine tuning, a type of "right to be deleted" in the USA would go a long way towards restoring some of the anonymity and privacy that we all enjoyed before Google decided no-one should ever forget. Of course Google, as they have already done in public debates, will spout off all kinds of excuses and claim this is "censorship." Google and other search engines are self-interested parties, more interested in what's good for their business than for the interests of individuals. Their claims of "censorship" are more like a smokescreen.

As in the European Union, there needs to be a balance between the public interest and requests for deletion, especially for public figures. However, in the case of non-public figures there should be more leeway, especially after the lapse of time and where old information is no longer accurate. The right to be deleted would give us all more power over deleting information about ourselves that in many cases we didn't put online ourselves and is not totally accurate.

National Data Breach Legislation
We urgently require a Federally mandated national data breach notification law that informs consumers in a timely manner when their personal details have been leaked. While many states have their own versions of this legislation already enacted, a national standard, as proposed by President Obama,[129] would make it easier for businesses to comply and easier to punish those that don't.

At the time of writing this book, The Data Security and Breach Notification Act of 2015[130] is busy working its way through Congress as more recognition grows for the need of this legislation. Hopefully, agreement can be reached on this act as many similar proposals have failed in the past.

Make Privacy a Political Issue
To make progress in this regard, we must make our privacy a political issue. We must all get involved and make our voices heard.

It doesn't matter which political party you support, we should make all political representatives aware that privacy matters as much as security does. The majority of political leaders are not opposed to these ideas, but they are not aware that we, the people, are concerned about them enough. Politicians want to get elected and re-elected—make them aware this is of concern and they will act. Make them understand we expect them to take this seriously and many will. If we don't speak up, the data brokering and advertising industry will continue to lobby in order to keep the status quo.

It's time, we the people, do something about privacy! Without privacy, you can't have freedom. And without freedom, democracy doesn't exist. Privacy is that important!

Parting Comments

If you have read this book and taken action on all the points mentioned, well done! Your systems and your personal data will be more secure and you will have secured your privacy a great deal more than most.

The world is becoming ever more connected. Unfortunately, new threats to your privacy and data security will emerge; new system and application vulnerabilities will be discovered and exploited. Governments and technology will become even more intrusive and try to invade new areas of our private lives.

To counter these threats, new privacy and cyber security products and solutions will be developed. It will be necessary to stay informed. Be sure to look out for the next, updated edition of this book and others by the author at www.johnberryauthor.com

Acknowledgements

Although only the author's name appears on the cover, writing any book is a team effort. I am extremely grateful for my family and friends who have supported and encouraged me during the writing of Hack Proof.

I am deeply grateful to my wife Mel who deserves special thanks for her overall enthusiasm, her words of advice, insightful comments, constructive criticism, book editing, grammar checking and other invaluable help throughout the entire writing process.

I also owe special thanks to Sheryl Thornburg for the cover design and for putting up with my many changes. Likewise I would like to extend my thanks to Deb Williams for her well-chosen and thoughtful editing skills. I must also thank and mention Mark Hornby and Rene Page for their marketing ideas and insight.

Several people were enormously helpful with reviewing potions of the text and providing feedback including my good friends Dr. Tom Barrett and author and business speaker, Jim Collins.

Lastly I also wish to express my appreciation to the following for their valuable technical feedback and information provided at various times during the writing of this book, Alexei Miagkov, Gary Ulaner, Kevin Haley and Kevin Mullenex.

John Berry is a technology executive with over 25 years experience working with cyber security systems. He is an author, writer, speaker, and consultant and has been involved with several start-ups as well as market leaders like Symantec and IBM.

John has travelled extensively, lived and worked in countries in Europe, the Middle East, Africa, and North America. He currently resides in Southern Florida.

Contact Information

Feedback and Comments

We hope you found this book insightful and the suggested action steps useful. We love to hear from our readers. If you would like to send any comments or suggestions, please do so via the website below.

Speaking

To have John speak at an event, or to conduct a cyber security or privacy briefing please contact us at our website.

www.johnberryauthor.com

All online references accessed and verified as correct and working in late 2015, however are subject to change or deletion. If any links are not working, try searching using the name of the article for an alternative link.

[1] Philip Messing, Jamie Schram, Bruce Golding, *Teen says he*

[2] Schmidt, Michael and Cooper, Helene, *ISIS Urges Sympathizers to kill US service members it identifies on website, The New York Times,* March 21, 2015,
http://www.nytimes.com/2015/03/22/world/middleeast/isis-urges-sympathizers-to-kill-us-service-members-it-identifies-on-website.html

[3] Rogier Creemers, *Planning Outline for the Construction of a Social Credit System (2014 – 2020),* China Copyright and Media, April 25, 2015,
https://chinacopyrightandmedia.wordpress.com/2014/06/14/planning-outline-for-the-construction-of-a-social-credit-system-2014-2020/

[4] Freedom House, *Freedom on the Net,* 2014,
https://freedomhouse.org/report/freedom-net/freedom-net-2014

[5] Mary Madden and Lee Raine, *Americans Attitudes about Privacy, Security and Surveillance,* Pew Research Center, May 2010, 2015,
http://www.pewinternet.org/2015/05/20/americans-attitudes-about-privacy-security-and-surveillance/

[6] Elizabeth Snell, *How does data de-identification affect clinical research*, July 30, 2015, Health IT Security,
http://healthitsecurity.com/news/how-does-data-de-identification-affect-clinical-research

[7] Andrew Perrin, Maeve Duggan, *American Internet Access: 2000-2015,* June 26, 2015, Pew Research Center,
http://www.pewinternet.org/2015/06/26/americans-internet-access-2000-2015/

[8] Ron Miller, *Cheaper sensors will fuel the age of smart everything,* March 10, 2015, Tech Crunch, http://techcrunch.com/2015/03/10/cheaper-sensors-will-fuel-the-age-of-smart-everything/

[9] Michael Lesk, *How much information is there in the world?,* 1997, http://www.lesk.com/mlesk/ksg97/ksg.html

[10] Webopedia staff, *How much Data is out there?* January 06, 2014, http://www.webopedia.com/quick_ref/just-how-much-data-is-out-there.html

[11] Sean Valant, *Infographic: A day in the Life of the Internet*, May 02, 2013, http://www.hostgator.com/blog/2013/05/02/a-day-in-the-life-of-the-internet/

[12] Steve Ambrose, There's a cyber surveillance arms race raging in the third world, The Daily Caller, October 15, 2015, http://dailycaller.com/2015/10/15/theres-a-cyber-surveillance-arms-race-raging-in-the-third-world/

[13] Jamie Dettmer, *Digital jihad: Isis, Al Qaeda seek a cyber caliphate to launch attacks on US*, Fox News, September 10, 2014, http://www.foxnews.com/world/2014/09/10/digital-jihad-isis-al-qaeda-seek-cyber-caliphate-to-launch-attacks-on-us/

[14] Antony Loewenstein, *The ultimate goal of the NSA is total population control,* July 10, 2014, *The Guardian*, http://www.theguardian.com/commentisfree/2014/jul/11/the-ultimate-goal-of-the-nsa-is-total-population-control

[15] John Walcott, Chinese espionage campaign targets US space technology, April 18, 2012, Bloomberg Business, http://www.bloomberg.com/news/articles/2012-04-18/chinese-espionage-campaign-targets-u-s-space-technology

[16] Jason Mick, Chinese hackers score F-35, Black hawk chopper and Patriot Missile data, May 28, 2013, Daily Tech,

http://www.dailytech.com/Chinese+Hackers+Score+F35+Black+Hawk+Chopper+and+PATRIOT+Missile+Data/article31638.htm

[17] Sharif Sakr, *Chinese cyber spies charged with stealing secrets from US companies,* May 19, 2014, Engadget,
http://www.engadget.com/2014/05/19/doj-charges-chinese-cyberspies-with-stealing-trade-secrets/

[18] Ben Elgin, Michael Riley, *Now at the Sands casino, an Iranian hacker in every server,* December 11, 2014, Bloomberg Business,
http://www.bloomberg.com/bw/articles/2014-12-11/iranian-hackers-hit-sheldon-adelsons-sands-casino-in-las-vegas

[19] *Europol chief warns on computer encryption,* BBC News website, March 22, 2015, http://www.bbc.com/news/technology-32087919

[20] Office of the High Commissioner for Human Rights, *Report on encryption, anonymity and the human rights framework,* United Nations Human Rights, June 2015,
http://www.ohchr.org/EN/Issues/FreedomOpinion/Pages/CallForSubmission.aspx

[21] *BlackBerry believes in encryption backdoors – believes it's good for business,* Bitdefender Business Insights,
http://businessinsights.bitdefender.com/blackberry-believes-encryption-backdoors-business

[22] Craig Timberg, *Newest Androids will join iPhones in offering default encryption, blocking police, The Washington Post,* September 8, 2014,
http://www.washingtonpost.com/blogs/the-switch/wp/2014/09/18/newest-androids-will-join-iphones-in-offering-default-encryption-blocking-police/

[23] Kashmir Hill, *FBI Director says Apple and Google Are Putting Their Customers "Beyond the Law",* Forbes, October 12, 2014,
http://www.forbes.com/sites/kashmirhill/2014/10/13/fbi-director-says-apple-and-google-are-putting-their-customers-beyond-the-law

[24] Ken Gude, *The FBI is dead wrong: Apple's encryption is clearly in the public interest*, Wired, October 17, 2014,
http://www.wired.com/2014/10/fbi-is-wrong-apple-encryption-is-good/

[25] Robert Barnes, *Supreme Court says police must get warrants for most cellphone searches, The Washington Post*, June 25, 2014,
http://www.washingtonpost.com/national/supreme-court-police-must-get-warrants-for-most-cellphone-searches/2014/06/25/e2ff1326-fc6b-11e3-8176-f2c941cf35f1_story.html

[26] James Comey, *Encryption, Public safety and "going dark"*, July 6, 2015, Lawfare,
http://www.lawfareblog.com/encryption-public-safety-and-going-dark

[27] Alex Hern, *Hacking Team hacked; firm sold spying tools to repressive regimes, documents claim,* July 6, 2015, *The Guardian*,
http://www.theguardian.com/technology/2015/jul/06/hacking-team-hacked-firm-sold-spying-tools-to-repressive-regimes-documents-claim

[28] USA Network *"Nation under A-hack" survey results,* June 24, 2015, http://www.thefutoncritic.com/news/2015/06/23/usa-network-nation-under-a-hack-survey-results-30313/20150623usa01/

[29] Shankar Vedantam, *To read all those web privacy policies, just take a month off work,* NPR all tech considered, April 19, 2012,
http://www.npr.org/blogs/alltechconsidered/2012/04/19/150905465/to-read-all-those-web-privacy-policies-just-take-a-month-off-work

[30] Aleecia M. McDonald and Lorrie Faith Cranor, *The cost of reading privacy policies*, I/S: A Journal of Law and Policy for the Information Society, 2008 Privacy Year in Review issue,
http://lorrie.cranor.org/pubs/readingPolicyCost-authorDraft.pdf

[31] Nate Anderson, *"Anonymized" data really isn't – and here's why not.* September 8, 2009, ARS Technica, http://arstechnica.com/tech-policy/2009/09/your-secrets-live-online-in-databases-of-ruin/

[32] *Community Health Systems data hack hits 4.5million*, BBC News Technology, August 18, 2014,
http://www.bbc.com/news/technology-28838661

[33] Brian Krebs, *We take your privacy and security. Seriously.* Krebs on Security, September 14, 2014,
http://krebsonsecurity.com/2014/09/we-take-your-privacy-and-security-seriously/

[34] Adam Greenberg, *Professor says Google search, not hacking, yielded medical info, SC Magazine,* August 29, 2014,
http://www.scmagazine.com/professor-says-google-search-not-hacking-yielded-medical-info/article/368909/

[35] Erik Holm, Leslie Scism, *MBIA says server of its Cutwater Unit "may have been illegally accessed", The Wall Street Journal,* October 7, 2014,
http://blogs.wsj.com/moneybeat/2014/10/07/mbia-says-server-of-its-cutwater-unit-may-have-been-illegally-accessed/

[36] Sophia Yan, *310,000 University of Maryland records hacked,* February 19, 2014, CNN Money,
http://money.cnn.com/2014/02/19/news/university-maryland-hack/

[37] Jose Pagliery, *Auburn University exposed its students Social Security numbers,* April 8, 2015, CNN Money,
http://money.cnn.com/2015/04/08/technology/security/auburn-data-breach/

[38] Maeve Duggan, *Online Harassment,* October 22, 2014, Pew Research Center, http://www.pewinternet.org/2014/10/22/online-harassment/

[39] Bruce Schneier, *Organizational Doxing,* July 10, 2015, Schneier on Security,
https://www.schneier.com/blog/archives/2015/07/organizational_.html

[40] Lisa Vaas, *Data-stealing botnets found in major data brokers servers,* September 26, 2013, Naked Security, https://nakedsecurity.sophos.com/2013/09/26/data-stealing-botnets-found-in-major-public-record-holders-servers/

[41] Christopher Seward, *LexiNexis says it had data breach earlier this year,* September 26, 2013, Phys. Org. News, http://phys.org/news/2013-09-lexisnexis-breach-earlier-year.html

[42] Eduard Kovacs, *Dun & BradStreet starts notifying customers of data breach,* October 29, 2013, Softpedia, http://news.softpedia.com/news/Dun-Bradstreet-Starts-Notifying-Customers-of-Data-Breach-395124.shtml

[43] Reuters, *Experian plc, Acquisition of Court Ventures Inc,* March 9, 2012, http://www.reuters.com/article/2012/03/09/idUS94865+09-Mar-2012+RNS20120309

[44] *Vietnamese National sentenced to 13 years in prison for operating a massive international hacking and identity theft scheme,* July 14, 2015, Information Week, Dark reading, http://www.darkreading.com/vietnamese-national-sentenced-to-13-years-in-prison-for-operating-a-massive-international-hacking-and-identity-theft-scheme/d/d-id/1321301

[45] Democratic Press Office, *What Information do Data brokers have on consumers and how do they use it,* December 18, 2013, U.S. Senate Committee on Commerce, Science & Transportation webcast, http://www.commerce.senate.gov/public/index.cfm?p=Hearings&ContentRecord_id=a5c3a62c-68a6-4735-9d18-916bdbbadf01&ContentType_id=14f995b9-dfa5-407a-9d35-56cc7152a7ed&Group_id=b06c39af-e033-4cba-9221-de668ca1978a

[46] Tim Barker, *Not dead yet: St. Louis woman sues credit reporting firms for declaring her deceased*, July 31, 2015, http://www.stltoday.com/business/local/not-dead-yet-st-louis-woman-sues-credit-reporting-firms/article_a0a03908-f8a1-5e52-9067-73365038bac6.html

[47] *Section 319 of the Fair and Accurate Credit Transactions Act of 2003: Fifth interim FTC report to Congress concerning the accuracy of information in credit reports,* December 2012, Federal Trade Commission, https://www.ftc.gov/reports/section-319-fair-accurate-credit-transactions-act-2003-fifth-interim-federal-trade

[48] *Cyber crime statistics and trends* (Infographic), May 17, 2013, Go-Gulf, http://www.go-gulf.com/blog/cyber-crime/

[49] *The Mind of a Cyber criminal,* December 1, 2010, Lloyds.com, http://www.lloyds.com/news-and-insight/news-and-features/emerging-risk/emerging-risk-2010/the-mind-of-a-cyber-criminal

[50] Mark Milian, *Top Ten Hacking Countries,* April 23, 2013, Bloomberg Business, http://www.bloomberg.com/slideshow/2013-04-23/top-ten-hacking-countries.html#slide1

[51] Stephan Cobb, *Cyber crime as a market,* May 9, 2015, *SC Magazine,* http://www.scmagazine.com/cyber-crime-as-a-market/article/240378/

[52] Doug Drinkwater, *Cyber crime costs global economy £265 billion,* June 9, 2014, http://www.scmagazineuk.com/cybercrime-costs-global-economy-265-billion/article/354644/

[53] 2015 Trustwave Global Security Report, https://www2.trustwave.com/rs/815-RFM-693/images/2015_TrustwaveGlobalSecurityReport.pdf

[54] Dancho Danchev, *DIY malware cryptor as a web service spotted in the wild,* February 22, 2013, Webroot Threat blog, http://www.webroot.com/blog/2013/02/22/diy-malware-cryptor-as-a-web-service-spotted-in-the-wild/

[55] Robert Windrem, *China read emails of top US Officials,* August 10, 2015, NBC News, http://www.nbcnews.com/news/us-news/china-read-emails-top-us-officials-n406046

[56] Violet Blue, *CryptoLocker's crime wave: A trail of millions in laundered Bitcoin,* December 22, 2013, ZD Net,

http://www.zdnet.com/article/cryptolockers-crimewave-a-trail-of-millions-in-laundered-bitcoin/

[57] *Ransomware on the rise*, The FBI, January 2015, https://www.fbi.gov/news/stories/2015/january/ransomware-on-the-rise/ransomware-on-the-rise

[58] Ian Steadman, *The Russian underground economy has democratized cyber crime,* November 12, 2015, Wired Magazine, http://www.wired.co.uk/news/archive/2012-11/02/russian-cybercrime

[59] Jane Wakefield, *Yahoo malware enslaves PCs to Bitcoin mining*, January 8, 2014, BBC News/ Technology http://www.bbc.com/news/technology-25653664

[60] Steven Musil, *Bitcoin-mining malware reportedly found on Google Play,* April 24, 2014, CNET, http://www.cnet.com/news/Bitcoin-mining-malware-reportedly-discovered-at-google-play/

[61] Lucian Constantin, *Bitcoin mining malware spreading on Skype, researcher says,* April 5, 2014. *PC World*, http://www.pcworld.com/article/2033287/Bitcoin-mining-malware-spreading-on-skype-researcher-says.html

[62] June 2015 Threat Stats, *SC Magazine*, http://www.scmagazine.com/june-2015-threat-stats/slideshow/2654/#0

[63] Slawomir Grzonkowski, Password recovery scam tricks users into handing over email account access, June 16, 2015, Symantec Connect blog, http://www.symantec.com/connect/blogs/password-recovery-scam-tricks-users-handing-over-email-account-access

[64] Identity Theft Resource Center, report date July 28, 2015, http://www.idtheftcenter.org/images/breach/ITRCBreachReport2015.pdf

[65] Dan Goodin, *8 million leaked passwords connected to LinkedIn, dating website*, June 6, 2012, ARS Technica,

http://arstechnica.com/security/2012/06/8-million-leaked-passwords-connected-to-linkedin/

[66] Nicole Perlroth and David Gelles, *Russian hackers amass over a billion Internet passwords.* August 5, 2014, *New York Times,* http://www.nytimes.com/2014/08/06/technology/russian-gang-said-to-amass-more-than-a-billion-stolen-internet-credentials.html

[67] Iulia Ion, Rob Reeder, Sunny Consolvo, *New Research: Comparing how security experts and non-security experts stay safe online,* July 23, 2015, Google Online Security Blog, http://googleonlinesecurity.blogspot.com/2015/07/new-research-comparing-how-security.html

[68] Ashley Carman, *Thousands of vulnerabilities identified in government system,* July 16, 2015, *SC Magazine,* http://www.scmagazine.com/department-of-the-interior-system-riddled-with-critical-vulnerabilities/article/426902/

[69] The Bug Bounty List, https://bugcrowd.com/list-of-bug-bounty-programs/

[70] Ashley Carman, *Yahoo bug bounty program pays out more than £1 million to researchers,* July 29, 2015, *SC Magazine,* http://www.scmagazine.com/ramses-martinez-publishes-yahoo-blog-post-on-vulnerability-research/article/429280/

[71] Dennis Fisher, *Vupen founder launches new zero-day acquisition firm Zerodium,* July 24, 2015, ThreatPost, https://threatpost.com/vupen-launches-new-zero-day-acquisition-firm-zerodium/113933

[72] IBM X-Force Threat Intelligence reports http://www-03.ibm.com/security/xforce/downloads.html

[73] Malware statistics, July 11, 2015, AV Test, https://www.av-test.org/en/statistics/malware/

[74] Fahmida Y. Rashid, *Anti-virus better at detecting email malware than web threats.* May 25, 2013, *PS Magazine/ SecurityWatch.* http://securitywatch.pcmag.com/apps-and-websites/309586-anti-virus-better-at-detecting-email-malware-than-web-threats

[75] Sara Peters, *The State of Apple Security,* October 14, 2015, Dark Reading, http://www.darkreading.com/endpoint/the-state-of-apple-security/d/d-id/1322560

[76] Independent tests of anti-virus software (Mac Reviews/ Tests) – July/ August 2014, AV Comparatives, http://www.av-comparatives.org/mac-security-reviews/

[77] http://truecrypt.sourceforge.net

[78] Sourabh, *How much email do we use daily? 182.9 billion emails sent/ received per day worldwide.* February 19, 2014, Source Digit.com
http://sourcedigit.com/4233-much-email-use-daily-182-9-billion-emails-sentreceived-per-day-worldwide/

[79] Radu Marinas, *Romanian hacker Guccifer appeals against arrest,* January 24, 2014, Reuters, http://www.reuters.com/article/2014/01/24/us-usa-hacking-guccifer-idUSBREA0N13S20140124

[80] *New York City Private Investigator who hacked into email accounts sentenced in Manhattan federal court to three months in prison.* June 26, 2015, FBI Press release, https://www.fbi.gov/newyork/press-releases/2015/new-york-city-private-investigator-who-hacked-into-email-accounts-sentenced-in-manhattan-federal-court-to-three-months-in-prison

[81] Jude McColgan, *Avast study exposes global WiFi browsing activity,* March 2, 2015, Avast! Blog, https://blog.avast.com/2015/03/02/avast-study-exposes-global-wi-fi-browsing-activity/

[82] Kristen Purcell, Joanna Brenner, Lee Rainie, *Search Engine use 2012,* March 9, 2012, Pew Research Center, http://www.pewinternet.org/2012/03/09/search-engine-use-2012/

[83] Nate Anderson, *Why Google keeps your data forever, tracks you with ads,* May 8, 2010, ARS Technica, http://arstechnica.com/tech-

policy/2010/03/google-keeps-your-data-to-learn-from-good-guys-fight-off-bad-guys/

[84] Chris Soghoian, *Debunking Google's log anonymization propaganda,* September 11, 2008, CNET, http://www.cnet.com/news/debunking-googles-log-anonymization-propaganda/#!

[85] Paul Ohm, *Broken Promises of Privacy: Responding to the surprising failure of anonymization,* August 13, 2009, University of Colorado Law school, http://papers.ssrn.com/sol3/papers.cfm?abstract_id=1450006

[86] *Online Health Searches aren't always confidential,* June 8, 2015, NPR All Tech Considered, http://www.npr.org/sections/alltechconsidered/2015/06/08/4128 93469/online-health-searches-arent-always-confidential

[87] Ashkan Soltani, Andrea Peterson, Barton Gellman, *NSA uses Google cookies to pinpoint targets for hacking,* December 10, 2013, *The Washington Post,* https://www.washingtonpost.com/blogs/the-switch/wp/2013/12/10/nsa-uses-google-cookies-to-pinpoint-targets-for-hacking

[88] Julia Angwin, *Meet the Online Tracking device that is virtually impossible to stop,* July 21, 2014, ProPublica, http://www.propublica.org/article/meet-the-online-tracking-device-that-is-virtually-impossible-to-block

[89] *Sites with canvas fingerprinting scripts as of May 1-5, 2014,* https://securehomes.esat.kuleuven.be/~gacar/sticky/index.html

[90] Gunes Acar, Christian Eubank, Steven Englehardt, Marc Juarez, Arvind Narayanan, Claudia Diaz, *The web never forgets: persistent tracking mechanisms in the wild,* KU Leuven, Esat/Cosic, iMinds & Princeton University, https://securehomes.esat.kuleuven.be/~gacar/persistent/the_w eb_never_forgets.pdf

[91] Gartner Group, *Gartner says mobile app stores will see annual downloads reach 102 billion in 2013,* September 19, 2013 http://www.gartner.com/newsroom/id/2592315

[92] Natasha Singer and Mike Isaac, *Uber data collection changes should be banned, privacy group urges,* June 22, 2015, *The New York Times*, http://www.nytimes.com/2015/06/23/technology/uber-data-collection-changes-should-be-barred-privacy-group-urges.html

[93] Jack Gillum, Stephan Braun, *Lawmaker with lavish décor billed private planes, concerts*, February 23, 2015, http://bigstory.ap.org/article/e2f1f52c3eb34caca7d74e5bf90f27f9/lawmaker-lavish-decor-billed-private-planes-concerts

[94] Timo Luege, *What human rights organizations can learn from fugitive John MacAfee,* Social Media for Good, January 9, 2013, http://sm4good.com/2013/01/09/ngo-learn-fugitive-john-mcafee/

[95] Aaron Smith, *US Smartphone Use in 2015,* April 1, 2015, Pew Research Center, http://www.pewinternet.org/2015/04/01/us-smartphone-use-in-2015/

[96] Rene Millman, *Updated: 97% of malicious mobile malware targets Android,* June 26, 2015, *SC Magazine*, http://www.scmagazineuk.com/updated-97-of-malicious-mobile-malware-targets-android/article/422783/2

[97] Eset report: *Apps on Google Play Steal Facebook credentials,* July 9, 2015, Eset Press release, http://www.eset.com/int/about/press/articles/malware/article/eset-report-apps-on-google-play-steal-facebook-credentials/

[98] Lukas Stefanko, *Porn clicker keeps infecting apps on Google Play,* July 23, 2015, http://www.welivesecurity.com/2015/07/23/porn-clicker-keeps-infecting-apps-on-google-play/

[99] Graham Cluley, *Bogus anti-virus apps in the official Windows and Android App stores,* May 15, 2014, Graham Cluley, https://grahamcluley.com/2014/05/bogus-anti-virus-apps-official-windows-phone-android-app-stores/

[100] Jaikumar Vijayan, *Flashlight app vendor settles with FTC over privacy violations,* December 6, 2013, *Computerworld*,

http://www.computerworld.com/article/2486577/application-security/flashlight-app-vendor-settles-with-ftc-over-privacy-violations.html

[101] Lucas Matney, *Report suggests young people may abandon social media if privacy breaches continue,* June 25. 2015, TechCrunch, http://techcrunch.com/2015/06/24/report-suggests-young-people-may-abandon-social-media-if-privacy-breaches-continue

[102] *Twitter blocks Jihadist group ISIS-affiliated accounts,* OSM, August 19, 2014, http://www.onlinesocialmedia.net/20140819/twitter-blocks-jihadist-group-isis-affiliated-accounts/

[103] *A New Threat to Children's Online Privacy: Parents,* PR Newswire, May 12, 2015, http://www.prnewswire.com/news-releases/a-new-threat-to-childrens-online-privacy-parents-300080557.html

[104] Tim Peterson, *Facebook to start telling brands who's talking about what topics,* March 10, 2015, *Advertising Age,* http://adage.com/article/digital/facebook-opens-topic-data-brands-datasift-deal/297507/

[105] Matt Petronzio, *How much is the average Facebook user worth?* Mashable, April 24, 2014, http://mashable.com/2014/04/24/facebook-average-worth-chart/

[106] Henry Farrell, *Facebook wasn't great at respecting privacy in the first place. It's gotten much worse.* August 18, 2015, *The Washington Post,* http://www.washingtonpost.com/blogs/monkey-cage/wp/2015/08/18/facebook-wasnt-great-at-respecting-privacy-in-the-first-place-its-gotten-much-worse/

[107] Reza Moaiandin, *Facebook: Please fix this security loophole before it's too late,* August 4, 2015, Salt Agency blog, https://salt.agency/blog/facebook-security-loophole/

[108] Jade Burke, *The average house could have 500 smart devices by 2022,* PCR, September 8, 2014,

http://www.pcr-online.biz/news/read/homes-could-have-over-500-smart-devices-by-2022/034691

[109] Federal Bureau of Investigation, *Internet-of-Things poses opportunities for cyber crime,* Public Service Announcement, September 10,2015, http://www.ic3.gov/media/2015/150910.aspx

[110] Zeljka Zora, *IoT is full of gaping security holes, says Shodan creator*, Help Net Security, June 9, 2015, http://www.net-security.org/secworld.php?id=18488

[111] Laura Barnes, *80% of IoT devices raise privacy concerns, says HP*, PCR, August 4, 2014,
http://www.pcr-online.biz/news/read/80-of-iot-devices-raise-privacy-concerns-says-hp/034473

[112] Paul, *Symantec Warns: Worm can target Internet-of-Things,* December 2, 2013, The Security Ledger,
https://securityledger.com/2013/12/symantec-warns-worm-can-target-internet-of-things/

[113] Paul, *When the Internet of things Attacks! Parsing the IoT Botnet story,* January 21, 2014, The Security Ledger,
https://securityledger.com/2014/01/when-the-internet-of-things-attacks-parsing-the-iot-botnet-story/

[114] David Holmes, *Hacker Search engine becomes the new Internet of things search engine,* July 8, 2015, Security Week,
http://www.securityweek.com/hacker-search-engine-becomes-new-internet-things-search-engine

[115] Dave Lee, *Keyless cars increasingly targeted by thieves using computers,* BBC News, October 27, 2014,
http://www.bbc.com/news/technology-29786320

[116] Marco Vernocchi, Robin Murdoch, Bouchra Carlier, *2015 Accenture Digital Consumer Survey,*
http://cmtapps.accenture.com/pages/digital-trust/Accenture-5-Trends-Screenager2.pdf

[117] Nancy Gohring, *Tales from the Cloud*, CiteWorld,

http://www.citeworld.com/article/2450823/internet-of-things/appirio-fitbit-experiment.html?source=CITNLE_nlt_weekly_update_2014-07-10#tk.rss_bigdataanalytics

[118] Markus Selinger, *Test: Fitness Wristband Reveals data, June 22, 2015, AV-Test*, http://www.av-test.org/en/news/news-single-view/test-fitness-wristbands-reveal-data/

[119] *All smartwatches are vulnerable to attack, finds study*, July 24, 2015, *SC Magazine*,
http://www.scmagazine.com/all-smartwatches-are-vulnerable-to-attack-finds-study/article/428321

[120] Karl Thomas, *How secure is your smartwatch*, April 15, 2015, We live security – Eset blog,
http://www.welivesecurity.com/2015/04/15/secure-smartwatch/

[121] Office of the Privacy Commissioner of Canada, *Automated facial recognition in the Public and private sectors*, March 2013,
https://www.priv.gc.ca/information/research-recherche/2013/fr_201303_e.asp

[122] Mexico police dismantle video cameras installed by gang, BBC News, June 18, 2015,
http://www.bbc.com/news/world-latin-america-33181800

[123] Privacy Advocates Statement on NTIA Face Recognition Process, June 20, 2015, https://www.eff.org/document/privacy-advocates-statement-ntia-face-recognition-process

[124] Facial-recognition talks collapse over privacy issues, June 17, 2015, BBC News, http://www.bbc.com/news/technology-33159612

[125] Liz Klimas, Say Cheese! Some States put drivers license photos in facial recognition databases for law enforcement to use, June 17, 2013, *The Blaze*,
http://www.theblaze.com/stories/2013/06/17/say-cheese-some-states-put-drivers-license-photos-in-facial-recognition-database-for-law-enforcement-use/

[126] Lee Hutchinson, *iOS 8 to stymie trackers and marketers with MAC address randomization,* June 9, 2014,
http://arstechnica.com/apple/2014/06/ios8-to-stymie-trackers-and-marketers-with-mac-address-randomization/

[127] Alan Travis & Charles Arthur, EU *court backs "right to be forgotten': Google must amend results on request,* May 13, 2014, *The Guardian,*
http://www.theguardian.com/technology/2014/may/13/right-to-be-forgotten-eu-court-google-search-results

[128] Jeffery Rosen, *The Right to be Forgotten,* Stanford Law Review, February 13, 2012,
http://www.stanfordlawreview.org/online/privacy-paradox/right-to-be-forgotten

[129]Office of the Press Secretary, *Safeguarding American Consumers & families,* January 12, 2015, The White House,
https://www.whitehouse.gov/the-press-office/2015/01/12/fact-sheet-safeguarding-american-consumers-families

[130] *The Data Security and Breach notification act of 2015,* April 1, 2015, National Law Forum,
http://nationallawforum.com/2015/04/01/the-data-security-and-breach-notification-act-of-2015/

CPSIA information can be obtained
at www.ICGtesting.com
Printed in the USA
LVOW04s0705050616

491250LV00009B/73/P